seasonal baking

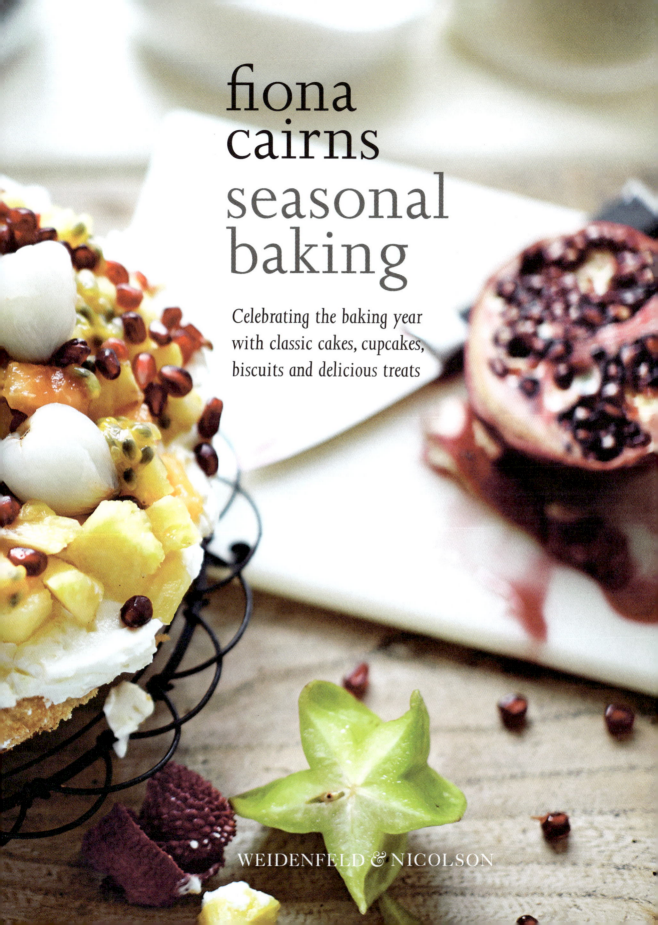

fiona
cairns
seasonal
baking

Celebrating the baking year
with classic cakes, cupcakes,
biscuits and delicious treats

WEIDENFELD & NICOLSON

for Rachel Eardley and all the
dedicated team at the bakery

contents

introduction

The rhythm and constancy of our ever-changing seasons has always been a joy to me. There is something to cherish in every month.

At the very beginning of the year, the anticipation of finding that first snowdrop nestled at the top of our garden, signalling that spring is on its way, never fails to lift my spirits.

Slowly, so very slowly, the days lengthen as we emerge from the dark winter months. The pale pink shoots of spring rhubarb appear in our shops, another hopeful sign that spring is gaining strength. The year goes on and the fruits of the soil reflect its progress: tiny broad beans, our English asparagus, followed by a colourful abundance of berries and fruits, roses in full bloom, blackberries in the hedgerows, a crisp pear… Our lives and the world around us are constantly changing, yet the year's progression is so reassuringly familiar.

This book is a celebration of that cycle. Each season brings its own mood and ingredients to enjoy and, of course, to use in our baking. Our calendar year is punctuated with celebrations, from Valentine's Day, to Easter, through summer picnics and holidays, to Hallowe'en and, of course, finally to Christmas. I have included plenty of recipes for each season; many are simple, and a few are more complicated cake decorating ideas, should you have the time and inclination.

Many of us already cook following the season, using produce at its very best, and that is usually grown locally. Sadly, due to the year-round availability of a lot of ingredients in our supermarkets, seasonality can be eclipsed; it can even be hard to tell what is in season. Should you choose to buy imported strawberries in the depths of winter, flown thousands of miles to a store near you, not only will you pay a premium, but you will find that they simply don't taste good. Neither will you have experienced the thrill of longing for them, followed by the sheer delight as you enjoy your eagerly awaited sweet strawberries in the summer months… it just makes sense and feels right.

I have always tried to cook and bake using the produce that each season has to offer. At the very start of the year, this includes the imported citrus and tropical fruits that are at their best while our British weather is at its coldest, and I make no apology for that.

In the summer months, though, my baking relies on Britain's plentiful harvest. I turn out airy sponges filled with seasonal berries and scattered with flowers, sometimes adding a floral hint of rose or lavender.

As the year moves on and we begin to crave warmth and comfort and turn to casseroles and warming soups, I love to bake moist, dark, spiced fruit cakes, or maybe a Blackberry, Apple and Cobnut Crumble Cake.

I developed and wrote the recipes, and the beautiful photographs were taken, in the centre of England on this journey through every month of the year. I simply wouldn't be tempted to bake a dark spiced Parkin in June, or a raspberry-spiked Peach Melba Gateau in December.

However, having said all this, please think of this book as a gentle guide to encourage you to use all that is the best from what each season has to offer, rather than as a manifesto. There are many recipes here that can be baked any time, any day. Make someone's special day that bit better and cook my Best Ever Chocolate Fudge Cake no matter what the season. Bake a batch of shortbreads (choose from 12 flavours), a Coffee, Cardamom and Walnut Cake or a tray of Peanut Butter and Sour Cherry Cookies whenever you have the urge.

I've enjoyed every minute of creating and writing this collection of recipes and hope you may find a few that become firm favourites you turn to summer after summer, or Christmas after Christmas.

Happy Seasonal Baking!

spring

spring cakes
new year resolutions
and pomegranate jewels

After the long, dark days and rich indulgences of December's festivities, we long for the light and freshness of spring to arrive. But the first calendar months are in the depths of our British winter. Spring, to my mind, should really be divided into 'winter spring' and 'summer spring'.

At the very beginning of the year – my 'winter spring' – we visit the gym with renewed intent and look for refreshing, sharper flavours and colours. This is the time to welcome the arrival in the shops of the magical pale pink spring rhubarb, grown by candlelight, and turn to the array of imported citrus and tropical fruits – all at their very best now – to brighten our days. This is when I love to bake Rhubarb and Vanilla Custard Cupcakes, Blood Orange, Lemon and Almond Cake and trays of Passion Fruit Kisses. In this chapter, you'll also find chocolate treats for Valentine's Day.

After the blossoms arrive, we slip into my 'summer spring'. If you are looking for recipes to bake for Mothering Sunday or Easter, here are delicious Classic Scones, Simnel Cake, Little Chocolate Egg Nests and Easter Rabbit Biscuits. As the days lengthen, our gardens come to life and everything seems somehow brighter, it's a great time to spend a few hours (or more!) baking and sharing the results.

rhubarb and vanilla custard cupcakes

This recipe is really in three parts. Both the rhubarb and the custard (actually French crème pâtissière) can be made well ahead, even the day before, and stored in the fridge. However, the cakes need to be assembled just before serving, or they will become soggy, and they won't travel well.

Crème pâtissière is to the baker a bit like chicken stock is to the chef: a very useful recipe to master and the basis for filling many cakes and tarts.

Makes 12

FOR THE CUPCAKES

175g self-raising flour

1 tsp baking powder

1 vanilla pod, seeds only, or
   2 tsp vanilla extract

175g golden caster sugar

175g unsalted butter, very soft,
   in small pieces

3 eggs, lightly beaten

FOR THE CRÈME PÂTISSIÈRE

1 vanilla pod, or 2 tsp
   vanilla extract

300ml whole milk

4 egg yolks

100g golden caster sugar

50g plain flour

a few knobs of unsalted butter

100ml double cream

To make the cakes, preheat the oven to 180°C/fan 160°C/350°F/ gas mark 4 and line a cupcake tray with 12 paper cases. I use a food mixer for this cake, but you could use a large bowl and a hand-held electric whisk, or a food processor.

Sift the flour and baking powder into the bowl. Split the vanilla pod lengthways, if using, and scrape the seeds into the bowl with the tip of a knife, or simply add the vanilla extract. Add the sugar, butter and eggs. Beat until well mixed, then divide between the cases. Bake for 15–17 minutes, or until the cakes are golden brown and spring back to the touch. Leave in the tin for a few minutes, then remove to a wire rack to cool completely.

To make the crème pâtissière, split the vanilla pod lengthways, if using, and scrape out the seeds with the tip of a knife. Place the pod and seeds in a saucepan with the milk and bring just to a boil. Remove from the heat, cover and leave for 10 minutes to infuse. If using vanilla extract, add it now.

In a food mixer (or using a bowl and a hand-held electric whisk), whisk together the egg yolks and sugar until pale, frothy and slightly thickened. Sift over the flour and mix it in thoroughly.

Remove the vanilla pod from the milk, if using, then reheat the milk until steaming, but not boiling. Pour about half on to the egg mixture, whisking as you do so.

FOR THE RHUBARB

Spring Rhubarb Compote
  (see page 15, you won't
  need it all), drained well
  on kitchen paper

TOOLS

apple corer (optional)
piping bag, no. 1 nozzle

Next, pour the egg mixture into the milk pan and, stirring constantly with a small whisk (scraping the sides down well), bring to a boil over a gentle heat. Cook for a couple of minutes, stirring constantly. The mixture will thicken into a custard. Pour into a clean bowl and dot with butter, to prevent a skin forming. Cover with cling film directly on the surface of the crème pâtissière and leave to cool down completely.

Whip the cream until slightly thickened. Loosen up the crème patissière by whisking it, then fold in the cream.

To assemble the cupcakes, remove the centre of each using an apple corer or a teaspoon and place one or two pieces of drained Spring Rhubarb Compote into the centre. Replace the cake 'plug'. Pipe a swirl of the crème patissière on each cake and decorate with another piece of drained rhubarb.

spring rhubarb compote

The gloriously bright pink stalks of forced rhubarb (grown by candlelight in Northern England) that appear in the first few months of the year feel like nothing short of a miracle, brightening the last dark days of early spring. This roasted rhubarb is a revelation: the pieces keep their shape and colour. Well drained, it makes the perfect accompaniment to Blood Orange, Lemon and Almond Cake, or to Sticky Lime and Coconut Loaf with Malibu Cream (see pages 58 and 57). You will also need it for the Rhubarb and Vanilla Custard Cupcakes (see page 12).

Serves 4

350g tender, pink spring
   rhubarb, cut into 3cm lengths
80g golden caster sugar,
   or Vanilla Sugar
   (see below right)
finely grated zest and juice of
   1 organic orange
1 tbsp orange blossom honey
   (optional)

Preheat the oven to 180°C/fan 160°C/350°F/gas mark 4.

Place the rhubarb, sugar, zest and juice in an ovenproof dish and mix gently with your fingers. Cover loosely with foil and bake for 30–40 minutes, or until the rhubarb is just softened and cooked, but still holding its shape. Drizzle with the honey, if using, and chill until required.

Try scattering the seeds of a pomegranate over the rhubarb compote, for an extra delicious and beautiful treat.

VANILLA SUGAR

Fill a jar with caster sugar and add a couple of vanilla pods. Seal and leave for at least a couple of weeks, for the flavours to develop. Now it's ready; top it up with more sugar as you use it up. I find this sugar is invaluable for baking, or for sprinkling on to cakes, biscuits and fruit.

thai rice and coconut cake

A most unusual, exotic cake, subtly scented with coconut, lemon grass, cardamom and jasmine rice. Thank you to Roz Denny for creating this cake and sharing it. After all the rich excesses of the festive season, this is especially delightful.

Serves 10

FOR THE CAKE

unsalted butter, for the tin

10 cardamom pods

250g Thai jasmine rice

750ml whole milk

1 lemon grass stalk, crushed

2 fresh bay leaves

125g white caster sugar

150ml whipping cream

150ml liquid coconut cream
   (not coconut milk)

6 eggs, separated

a few physalis (or other seasonal
   soft fruit), to serve

FOR THE TOPPING

200ml quark (low-fat soft
   cheese), or mascarpone

300ml double cream

1 tsp vanilla extract

finely grated zest of
   1 unwaxed lemon

30g caster sugar, or to taste

Preheat the oven to 180°C/fan 160°C/350°F/gas mark 4. Butter a 25cm round, deep cake tin and line the base and sides with baking parchment.

To de-seed the cardamom pods, split the husks with the point of a knife, empty all the little seeds into a mortar and grind them to a powder with the pestle. Sift to remove any pieces of husk.

Put the rice into a large saucepan of cold unsalted water, bring to a boil, then boil for three minutes. Drain.

Return the rice to the rinsed-out pan with the milk, lemon grass, cardamom powder and bay leaves. Add all but 1 tbsp of the sugar. Bring to a boil, then reduce the heat and simmer gently for 20 minutes, stirring occasionally. Allow to cool, still stirring occasionally, then remove the lemon grass and bay leaves.

Mix the whipping cream and coconut cream together and stir into the rice with the egg yolks. Whisk the egg whites until firm, then whisk in the remaining 1 tbsp of sugar until softly stiff. Fold into the rice mixture, and pour into the prepared tin.

Bake in the preheated oven for 35–45 minutes. The top should still wobble very slightly when shaken. Cool completely in the tin, then turn out on to a serving plate and remove the papers.

Loosen up the quark (or mascarpone) with a whisk, and lightly whip the double cream until just firm. Mix the two together with the vanilla, adding the lemon zest and sugar to taste. Spread over the top and sides of the cake, swirling with a palette knife.

Decorate with a few physalis (I twisted the leaves back up). This cake can be made a day ahead and stored in the fridge.

new year's resolution tropical jewel cake

Banish winter blues with this very simple, light, butter-free sponge cake laced with a lime syrup, sandwiched with a creamy ginger filling and topped with an abundance of exotic fruits. The cake is fat free, and the filling is based on quark, a very low-fat cheese (though use a lightly whipped cream, or mascarpone, if you prefer). It is really refreshing and looks stunning. If you don't want to use exotic fruits, a layer of Spring Rhubarb Compote (see page 15), well drained on kitchen paper, would make a delicious substitute.

Serves 6–8

FOR THE SPONGE

vegetable oil, for the tin

3 eggs, lightly beaten

125g golden caster sugar

125g self-raising flour, sifted

FOR THE LIME SYRUP

finely grated zest and juice of
   2 limes (organic if possible)

120g golden caster sugar

FOR THE FILLING

2–3 tbsp ginger syrup (from the
   stem ginger jar)

2–3 stem ginger pieces, finely
   chopped

500g quark (or see recipe
   introduction)

800g exotic fruits of your
   choice, prepared weight
   (I used lychees, pomegranate,
   pineapple, passion fruit,
   papaya and star fruit)

Preheat the oven to 180°C/fan 160°C/350°F/gas mark 4. Oil two 20cm round cake tins and line the bases with baking parchment.

Warm the bowl and whisk attachment of your food mixer by standing both in hot water, then dry them thoroughly.

Whisk the eggs and sugar until the mixture resembles a creamy mousse. It will take five to six minutes to reach what is known as the 'ribbon stage': lift the whisk and drizzle a trail of mixture back into the bowl. You will see it standing proud for a few seconds before it sinks back into the rest. Using a metal spoon and a light hand, gently fold in the flour. Divide the batter between the tins.

Bake in the preheated oven for 15–20 minutes, or until a skewer comes out clean, or the cake springs back to the touch. Rest in the tins for a minute or so, then turn out and cool on a wire rack.

Meanwhile, to make the lime syrup, simply mix the lime zest and juice with the sugar in a small bowl.

Prepare the filling by mixing the ginger syrup and ginger into the quark until smooth.

When ready to serve, place one cake, flat base up, on a serving plate or cake stand and brush with half the lime syrup. Spread half the ginger filling over, then half the fruits. Place the other cake on top, flat base down (so the flat bases are together) and repeat, arranging the fruits on the top attractively.

pomegranate jewels in syrup

I can't get enough of the ruby-red, jewel-like pomegranates that brighten our early spring months. Choose fruits that are heavy for their size (they will be full of juice), with a glossy skin. Try this recipe, well drained, as an accompaniment to Lemon Madeira Cake (see page 41).

Makes a small bowlful

2 pomegranates

juice of 2 blood oranges, or other sweet oranges, plus 1 blood orange, peeled and sliced (organic, if possible)

40g caster sugar

a few mint leaves (optional)

Cut one of the pomegranates in half and squeeze it as you would an orange, to remove the juice. To make the pomegranate syrup, simply place the pomegranate and orange juices and sugar in a pan. Heat gently until the sugar dissolves, then increase the heat until the syrup is slightly thickened. Remove and cool a little, then strain through a nylon sieve to remove any pith, pulp or seeds.

Meanwhile, place the seeds from the second pomegranate in a serving bowl (ensuring you remove all the white pith) and add the sliced orange.

Pour over the syrup, mix together and chill for up to three days. Scatter with the mint leaves, if using, to serve.

zesty lemon and white chocolate cupcakes

These are really zingy, citrussy cakes. The sharpness of lemon combines so well with white chocolate. It's important to buy good white chocolate, as it makes a better icing; I prefer Swiss brands. The sponge recipe is the same as used for Rhubarb and Vanilla Custard Cupcakes (see page 12), but with added lemon.

Makes 12

FOR THE CAKES

175g self-raising flour, sifted

1 tsp baking powder

1 tsp vanilla extract

finely grated zest of 2 large
   unwaxed lemons

175g golden caster sugar

175g unsalted butter, really soft,
   in small pieces

3 eggs, lightly beaten

FOR THE FILLING

12 tsp Lemon Curd
   (see page 27)

FOR THE BUTTERCREAM

200g good-quality white
   chocolate, finely chopped

200g unsalted butter, very soft

TO DECORATE

12 fresh or crystallised violets
   (see page 74 for how to
   crystallise flowers)

TOOLS

apple corer (optional)

large piping bag, fitted with
   a star nozzle

Preheat the oven to 180°C/fan 160°C/350°F/gas mark 4 and line a cupcake cake tray with 12 paper cases.

Make the cake batter as for the Rhubarb and Vanilla Custard Cupcakes (see page 12), adding the lemon zest to the batter at the same time as the vanilla. Bake and cool as on page 12.

Once the cakes are cool, remove the centre of each using an apple corer or a teaspoon and place 1 tsp of lemon curd into the centre. Replace the cake 'plug'.

To make the buttercream, put the white chocolate into a heatproof bowl and stand it over barely simmering water, ensuring the bowl does not touch the water. Once melted, remove from the heat and allow to cool.

In a food mixer, or in a bowl using a hand-held electric whisk, cream the butter until light, then slowly add the cooled, melted chocolate. Chill slightly, then whisk to thicken. Fill the piping bag and pipe the buttercream on to the cupcakes. Decorate each with a dry, freshly picked violet, or a crystallised violet.

passion fruit curd

Choose ripe fruits, with crinkly skins. If yours are very juicy, or quite small, the yield will differ.

Makes about 390g jar

5 ripe passion fruits
juice of ½ lemon
150g golden caster sugar
50g unsalted butter, in pieces
2 large eggs, lightly beaten

Scoop the passion fruit pulp and seeds into a small saucepan with a teaspoon or two of water. Heat gently to loosen the seeds from the pulp, then press through a nylon sieve. Discard the seeds.

In a small heatproof bowl set over simmering water (make sure the bowl does not touch the water) place the passion fruit pulp, lemon juice, sugar and butter. Using a hand whisk (or wooden spoon if you prefer), stir until the butter has melted. Strain the eggs through a sieve into the mixture, and continue as for Lime Curd (see right), storing the curd in the same way.

lime curd

Even more delicious than lemon curd to my mind, this is wonderful as a filling in a Victoria sponge, or spread thickly on toast or scones. You can follow the same recipe to make lemon curd, using two unwaxed lemons instead of limes. Or even use two Seville oranges, or three blood oranges. Scrub the fruits well if you can't find unwaxed or organic citrus, or your curd will contain the wax coating.

Makes about 350g jar
**finely grated zest and juice of
    3 limes (organic, if possible)**
150g golden caster sugar
50g unsalted butter, in pieces
2 large eggs, lightly beaten

In a small heatproof bowl set over simmering water (make sure the bowl does not touch the water), place the zest and juice, sugar and butter. Using a hand whisk (or wooden spoon if you prefer), stir until the butter has melted. Strain the eggs through a sieve into the mixture, and, patiently, stir constantly for 20–30 minutes, until the curd thickens and thickly coats the back of a spoon.

Pour the curd into a sterilised jar with a non-metallic lid and seal. Stored in the fridge, the curd will keep for two weeks. After opening, it will keep for a week or so in the fridge, but is at its best when fresh.

TO STERILISE JARS AND BOTTLES
The easiest way to do this is to rinse the containers and lids thoroughly, place them upside down in the dishwasher and run a full cycle. Or preheat the oven to 150°C/fan 130°C/300°F/ gas mark 2. Wash the containers and lids in hot soapy water, then place in a tray of shallow water. Put in the oven for 15 minutes.

passion fruit kisses

I dare you to try stopping at just one… Fill the biscuits with Passion Fruit Curd (see page 26) instead of the cream filling here if you prefer. A great Valentine's day treat.

Makes 30 passion fruit 'sandwiches'

FOR THE BISCUITS

220g unsalted butter,
    softened, in pieces

80g icing sugar, sifted

220g plain flour, sifted,
    plus more to dust

100g ground almonds

FOR THE PASSION FRUIT FILLING

3 passion fruits, with ripe,
    crinkly skins

150g double cream

3 tbsp icing sugar, sifted,
    or to taste, plus more to dust

TOOLS

5cm heart-shaped cutter

Line two baking trays with baking parchment.

To make the biscuits, place the butter and icing sugar in the bowl of a food mixer (or use a large bowl and a hand-held electric whisk), and cream together well. Add the flour and ground almonds gradually, mixing between each addition, until the dough binds together. Wrap in cling film and chill for 30 minutes. Preheat the oven to 180°C/fan 160°C/350°F/gas mark 4.

Lightly flour a work top and roll out the dough to 3–4mm thick. Using the heart-shaped cutter, cut out the biscuits, close together, then re-roll and continue until all the dough is used. (I cut 60.) At this point, you can freeze the cut-out biscuits.

Place the biscuits, well spaced out, on the lined baking trays and bake in the preheated oven for 12–15 minutes.

Leave on the trays for a few minutes, then transfer to a wire rack to cool completely. The hearts will keep well for a few days in an airtight container, but of course are at their best freshly baked.

When ready to serve, cut the passion fruits in half and scoop the seeds and pulp into a bowl. Whip the double cream until thickened, fold in the passion fruit and sweeten to taste with the icing sugar. Use to sandwich the biscuits together. Dust with icing sugar to serve.

bitter-sweet chocolate heart biscuits

A wonderfully crisp chocolate biscuit that can be decorated as much or as little as you desire.

Makes 20–30

FOR THE BISCUITS

140g plain flour

40g cocoa, plus more to dust

pinch of salt

125g unsalted butter, softened

125g golden caster sugar

1 egg yolk

1 tbsp golden syrup

TO DECORATE (OPTIONAL)

100g icing sugar, or fondant
   icing sugar

pot of pink food colour paste

20g dark chocolate, melted

pot of hundreds and thousands

TOOLS

variety of heart-shaped cutters,
   about 5–8cm

Line two baking trays with baking parchment. Sift together the flour, cocoa and salt.

In a food mixer (or using a large bowl and a hand-held electric whisk), beat the butter and sugar until light and creamy. Add the egg yolk and syrup, then gradually the flour mixture, until you have a smooth dough. Wrap in cling film and chill for 30 minutes. Preheat the oven to 180°C/fan 160°C/350°F/gas mark 4.

Dust a work surface with cocoa and roll the dough out to 4–5mm thick. Using heart-shaped cutters, cut out the biscuits and place on the trays, keeping the smaller on one and the larger on the other. Re-roll to use all the dough; you should have 20–30. At this point, you can freeze the cut-out biscuits. Bake in the preheated oven for 10–12 minutes for small biscuits and 15–18 minutes for large. Leave on the tray for a couple of minutes, then transfer to a wire rack to cool completely.

For a simple finish, dust with cocoa and serve.

If you want to decorate the hearts, sift the icing sugar into a bowl. Add 2–3 tsp of water, little by little, stirring all the time until you have a good spreadable consistency like thick cream. Divide the icing between three bowls. Using the food colour paste, colour the icing three different shades of pink. Cover each with cling film until ready to use, as it dries out quite quickly.

Spread a little icing on each biscuit, using a teaspoon to ease it over the surface, or dip half a biscuit into the icing (if you used fondant icing sugar, it will be less likely to run off the biscuits). Leave a few plain and drizzle with chocolate, using the tines of a fork. You can flick the chocolate over a few pink iced biscuits and swirl with a cocktail stick or knife, in patterns. (You can also do this with contrasting icing colours.) Sprinkle with hundreds and thousands, if you like. Do all this before the icing sets, then allow to dry. They will keep for a few days in an airtight container.

chocolate love cake

Deceptively light, this is essentially a simple chocolate truffle cake to share with the one(s) you love. The recipe is based on one from the Tour D'Argent in Paris, no less. The trick is that the chocolate must be just melted and still hot when you pour it into the cream. You can bake the light sponge base (use the recipe on page 18, but you only need a very thin, 6–7mm layer of it), or simply buy a ready-made flan case and cut it to size. Once it is soaked in liqueur and syrup, it will be fine.

I've made this in a 20cm heart tin, but make it in a 20cm round tin if it's easier.

Serves 8

25g golden caster sugar

6–7mm-thick slice of sponge (see recipe introduction)

50ml brandy, or raspberry liqueur

220g 70% cocoa solids chocolate

450ml whipping cream

TO DECORATE

1 tbsp cocoa, to dust

fresh, dry, unsprayed red rose petals

First, dissolve the sugar with 25ml of water in a small saucepan over a gentle heat, then bring to a boil, reduce the heat and simmer for a couple of minutes. Leave to cool.

Now take a 20cm heart-shaped cake tin, or round springform tin. Line it with a thin cake card, or a piece of thin cardboard, cut to the same size as the tin. If using a springform tin, ensure the lip of the base is facing down, or it will be impossible to move the cake.

Place the sponge on a work top and press a chopping board gently on to it to flatten. Cut to fit the tin. Mix the sugar syrup with the alcohol and brush it all over the sponge. Place in the tin.

Using a serrated knife, chop the chocolate and place in a small bowl standing over very gently simmering water. Ensure the bowl is not touching the water. When it has just melted, remove from the heat. With a hand-held electric whisk and large mixing bowl, or a food mixer, lightly whip the cream until just beginning to thicken. Lightly stir the chocolate and, still whipping, pour the still-hot chocolate slowly on to the cream. Immediately pour into the tin, cover with cling film and leave overnight in the fridge.

When ready to serve, dip a knife in hot water and dry it, then immediately cut all around the edge of the tin. Remove the tin and move the cake on to a serving plate or cake stand.

Dust with a sprinkling of cocoa and a finish with a flourish of red rose petals.

banana and hazelnut breakfast muffins

Get everything ready the night before, all weighed up, cases in the tins, even make the crumble. In the morning simply mash the bananas, mix everything together and bake. It's a great way to wake the household to a delicious aroma on Mothering Sunday.

Makes 10–12

FOR THE TOPPING

EITHER

50g unsalted butter, cut into
  pieces and chilled

50g plain flour, sifted

50g oats

40g demerara sugar

OR

40g demerara sugar

FOR THE MUFFINS

50g hazelnuts or walnuts

200g plain flour

2 tsp baking powder

½ tsp bicarbonate of soda

1 tsp ground cinnamon

pinch of salt

160g golden caster sugar

4 small (or 3 large) over-ripe,
  black spotted bananas
  (about 300g peeled weight)

130g unsalted butter, melted
  and cooled

2 eggs, lightly beaten

1 tsp vanilla extract

4–5 tbsp whole milk

Make the topping first. To make the oat crumble, with your fingertips rub together the butter and flour in a bowl until they form crumbs, then stir in the oats and sugar. Otherwise, measure out the demerara sugar and put into a small bowl.

Preheat the oven to 180°C/fan 160°C/350°F/gas mark 4. Put the nuts on a baking tray and cook for five minutes, or until lightly roasted. Cool slightly, then chop. Place 12 muffin cases in a muffin tin. Sift together the flour, baking powder (to keep the muffins light), bicarbonate of soda, cinnamon and salt into a bowl. Stir in the caster sugar. In another large bowl, mash the bananas with a fork and add the butter, eggs and vanilla extract. Fold in the dry ingredients, then the nuts and finally the milk. Divide between the cases and top with either demerara sugar or oat crumble.

Bake for 20–25 minutes, or until they spring back to the touch, or a skewer comes out clean. Cool on a wire rack.

classic scones

A doddle to make, the secret to the perfect scone is to touch the dough as little as possible. Light, cool hands and quick work will result in delicious warm scones on the table in just 30 minutes. Scones taste best just baked, though any leftovers are delicious toasted for breakfast the next day.

Makes 8–10

80g unsalted butter, slightly chilled and cut into pieces, plus more for the tray

300g self-raising flour, plus more to dust

½ tsp baking powder

pinch of salt

50g golden caster sugar, plus more to sprinkle

170ml buttermilk (or 150ml whole milk), plus more if needed, and to glaze

TOOLS

6cm round or fluted cutter

Preheat the oven to 220°C/fan 200°C/425°F/gas mark 7. Lightly butter a baking tray.

Sift the flour, baking powder and salt into a large mixing bowl and stir in the sugar. Add the butter, cutting it into the flour mixture with a kitchen knife. With a light hand, rub in the butter until the mixture resembles fine breadcrumbs. Lift the mixture high as you work to incorporate air. Gradually add the buttermilk, again cutting it into the mixture until you have an even, soft dough (you may need a little more).

Turn the dough on to a work top lightly dusted with flour and pat out gently all over to a thickness of about 3cm. Working quickly with the cutter, cut out the scones as closely as you can, re-form the dough and cut out further scones (these won't rise as well, but will still taste delicious). Space out on the baking tray, brush with milk and sprinkle with sugar.

Bake in the preheated oven for 12–15 minutes, or until well-risen and golden.

Cool on a wire rack covered with a tea towel. These are best served just-warm, with clotted cream, unsalted butter and jam, for folks to help themselves. Oh, and a large pot of steaming tea, too.

CHEESE SCONES

Omit the sugar and add 1 tsp English mustard and 60g of grated cheddar cheese to the buttermilk or milk. Sprinkle the tops with a little extra cheese before baking.

Scones do freeze well, taking an hour or two to defrost. Reheat in the oven, wrapped in foil.

little cherry bakewell tarts

A plate of these will delight any mother (and child, too) and they're great fun to make. If you don't want to make the pastry, simply substitute with 200g of bought all-butter shortcrust pastry. It's worth making it though, as it gives more than you need, and the remainder freezes brilliantly.

Makes 12

FOR THE RICH SWEET PASTRY

100g unsalted butter, cut into
  pieces, chilled very slightly,
  plus more for the tin
200g plain flour, plus more
  to dust
pinch of salt
80g caster (or icing) sugar
1 egg yolk

FOR THE FILLING

100g ground almonds
100g unsalted butter, really soft,
  in pieces
100g golden caster sugar
finely grated zest of
  1 organic orange
1 egg, lightly beaten

FOR THE JAM AND DECORATION

6 tsp morello cherry or
  raspberry jam
100g icing sugar or fondant
  icing sugar, sifted
2–3 tsp lemon juice
12 red glacé cherries,
  rinsed and dried

TOOLS

7cm round cutter

Lightly butter a 12-hole bun tin, then flour each hole well, turning and tapping to remove excess flour.

Sift the flour and salt into a bowl and stir in the sugar. With your fingertips rub in the pieces of butter (or, if using a food processor, pulse-blend together). Add the egg yolk and 1–2 tbsp ice-cold water, or enough to make a smooth dough. Do not over-work, or you will toughen the pastry. Wrap in cling film and rest in the fridge for an hour or so.

On a lightly floured work top, roll out the pastry to about 3mm thick and cut out 12 rounds using the cutter. Press lightly into the holes of the tin. Chill for 30 minutes. Wrap and freeze the remaining pastry for another time.

Meanwhile, put the filling ingredients into a bowl and mix well. Preheat the oven to 190°C/fan 170°C/375°F/gas mark 5.

Place about ½ tsp of jam into the base of each tart case, then top with the filling. Bake in the preheated oven for 15–20 minutes, until lightly golden. Leave to cool in the tin for five minutes, then transfer to a wire rack to cool completely.

To ice the tarts, put the icing sugar in a bowl and stir in only enough lemon juice to make a smooth, spreadable icing. Spoon a little over each tart and top with a glacé cherry. Allow the icing to set, then serve.

lemon madeira cake

This is a quite delicious rich, damp, tangy lemon cake, based on an old recipe in a book my mother cooked from years ago. Serve on its own at any time, or as a dessert with a bowl of seasonal fruit.

Either the Spring Rhubarb Compote or Pomegranate Jewels in Syrup (both must be well drained, see pages 15 and 22), with a dollop of crème fraîche, would make a perfect accompaniment. As it is so moist, the cake keeps very well for a couple of days.

Serves 8

FOR THE CAKE

100g unsalted butter, melted and
    cooled, plus more for the tin
280g plain flour
2 tsp baking powder
pinch of salt
4 eggs, lightly beaten
300g golden caster sugar
finely grated zest and juice of
    1 unwaxed lemon
150ml double cream

FOR THE GLAZE AND ICING

3 tbsp apricot jam
100g icing sugar, sifted
1–2 tbsp lemon juice

Preheat the oven to 180°C/fan 160°C/350°F/gas mark 4. Butter a 20cm round, deep springform tin, and line the base and sides with baking parchment.

Sift the flour, baking powder and salt together and set aside.

Using a food mixer, or a bowl and hand-held electric whisk, beat the eggs, sugar and lemon zest until really light, fluffy and thickened. This may take five minutes or so.

With a large spoon gently fold in the cream, followed by the flour mixture and lastly the melted butter and lemon juice. When evenly mixed, tip into the prepared tin. Bake in the preheated oven for 55–60 minutes, or until a skewer comes out clean.

Cool the cake in the tin for a few minutes, then turn out to cool on a wire rack. When cold, slightly warm the apricot jam, push it through a sieve, then brush over the top and sides of the cake.

Put the icing sugar into a bowl and very gradually indeed add the lemon juice, mixing with a spoon all the while, until you have a smooth, pourable icing (don't make it too runny). Using a teaspoon, drizzle randomly over the top of the cake, as in the photo. Leave to set.

spring bonnets

These are so pretty and delicious too. Packed into a little box, they make a perfect gift for a mother, or even an Easter gift.

Makes about 20

FOR THE BISCUITS

250g unsalted butter, softened

100g golden caster sugar

250g plain flour, sifted, plus
   more to dust

pinch of salt

125g ground almonds

finely grated zest of 2 large
   unwaxed lemons

FOR THE ICING

500g icing sugar or fondant
   icing sugar, sifted, plus more
   if needed

5–6 tbsp lemon juice

pot of yellow food colour paste

TO DECORATE

tiny sugar flowers

20 x 15cm lengths of
   4mm-wide ribbon

TOOLS

large fluted (8cm) and small
   (4cm) round cutters

Line two baking trays with baking parchment. Put the butter and sugar into a food mixer (or use a large bowl and a hand-held electric whisk). Cream until fluffy, then add the flour, salt, ground almonds and zest. Wrap in cling film and chill for 30 minutes. Preheat the oven to 180°C/fan 160°C/350°F/gas mark 4.

On a lightly floured work top, roll out the dough to 4mm thick. Cut out circles: I used an 8cm-wide fluted cutter and a smaller 4cm circle cutter. Place the larger on one tray, the smaller on another, re-rolling until all the dough is used. You should have 20 of each size. At this point, you can freeze the cut-out biscuits. Bake in the preheated oven: the smaller biscuits take nine to 10 minutes and the larger 15–18 minutes. Cool for a few minutes on the trays, then remove to wire racks to cool completely. You can bake the biscuits a day or two ahead and store in an airtight container.

To make the icing, put the icing sugar in a bowl. Slowly stir in the lemon juice until you have a fairly stiff paste that will spread over the bonnets without pouring over the edges into a mess (using fondant icing sugar will prevent this). If needed, the icing can be thickened with more icing sugar or thinned out with water.

Divide between two bowls and stir enough yellow food colour into one to make pale yellow icing, leaving the other white. Cover each with cling film.

Take five larger biscuits, and place on a work top. Spread a small amount of white icing into the centre and top with a small biscuit (this is the crown of the bonnet). Spoon over some white icing and gently spread to the edge using a small blunt knife. Decorate straight away with sugar flowers and ribbon, sticking them to the still-tacky icing. Repeat. Do the same with the second half of the biscuits and the yellow icing, until all the bonnets have been decorated and half are white and half are yellow. Leave to set.

floral fancies

This is one large cake, cut into little shapes. I have iced them all in pale orange, but a variety of pastels would be equally pretty. If time is short, decorate with dragees or ready-made flowers instead. Fondant icing sugar helps stop the icing running off the cakes; if using it, omit the liquid glucose.

Makes 24–30, depending on size

FOR THE BLOSSOMS

100g white sugarpaste

icing sugar, to dust

FOR THE CAKE

unsalted butter, for the tin

5 eggs, separated

220g golden caster sugar

250g ground almonds

1 tsp baking powder

3–4 tbsp apricot jam

1–2 tsp orange flower water

FOR THE MARZIPAN

200g ground almonds

140g icing sugar, plus more
    to dust

140g golden caster sugar

2 drops of almond extract

1 tsp lemon juice

1 egg, lightly beaten

FOR THE ICING AND DECORATION

1–2 tsp orange flower water

1–2 tsp liquid glucose

750g icing sugar or fondant
    icing sugar, sifted

pot of orange food colour paste

30g bag royal icing, no. 1 nozzle

pot of edible sugar pearls

TOOLS

set of blossom plunger cutters
    6, 10 and 13mm

Roll out the sugarpaste thinly on a board dusted with icing sugar. Cut out blossoms with the cutters and leave for a few hours.

Preheat the oven to 180°C/fan 160°C/350°F/gas mark 4. Butter a 30 x 23cm Swiss roll tin and line with baking parchment. In a large bowl, using a hand-held electric whisk, whisk the egg whites until they form soft peaks. In another bowl, whisk the egg yolks and sugar for a minute or two; you don't want them too thick. Fold in the egg whites, ground almonds and baking powder.

Pour into the tin and bake for 20–25 minutes, until a skewer comes out clean. Leave to cool for a few minutes, then turn on to baking parchment laid over a wire rack. When the cake is cold, trim the top to make it level, than turn it upside down so the flat base is on top. Warm the jam in a small pan, then push through a sieve, add the flower water and brush it over the cake.

Make the marzipan (see page 50). On a work top dusted with icing sugar, roll it to the same size as the top of the cake. Lift over the cake, press down gently and trim the edges. Cut the cake into even-sized shapes (about 4cm); rounds, squares, diamonds, hearts, or rectangles. Chill for an hour, to make them easier to ice.

Gradually mix the flower water and glucose into the icing sugar, adding a little food colour and enough water to achieve a pale orange, thickish pouring consistency. Place the cakes on a wire rack and spoon over the icing, easing it down the sides with a teaspoon. (Using fondant icing sugar prevents it running off.)

Use the blossoms to decorate the cakes before the icing sets, or use the royal icing if it has set. Add the sugar pearls to the centre of the blossoms, sticking them on with royal icing. Pack into little paper cases; they keep well for a few days. Do not keep in the fridge or in an airtight container, or they will 'sweat'.

almond-apricot pansy cake

A wonderful cake to serve for tea, or as a dessert. It would be equally good with a blackcurrant or cherry jam (or see pages 106–109 for some ideas for home-made jams). I have decorated it with pansies on top, but primroses, violets or a mixture would be equally pretty.

Serves 8

FOR THE CAKE

225g unsalted butter, really soft,
  plus more for the tins
160g self-raising flour
1 tsp baking powder
60g ground almonds
225g golden caster sugar
4 eggs, lightly beaten
1 tsp almond extract
finely grated zest of 1 organic
  orange and juice of ½

FOR THE FILLING AND
DECORATION

200g crème fraîche
5 tbsp best-quality apricot jam
icing sugar, to dust
freshly picked, dry, unsprayed
  pansies

Preheat the oven to 180°C/fan 160°C/350°F/gas mark 4. Butter two 20cm round tins and line the bases with baking parchment.

Sift the flour and baking powder into a bowl, stir in the ground almonds and set aside.

Put the softened butter and sugar into the bowl of a food mixer (or use a bowl and a hand-held electric whisk) and cream together until light and fluffy. Gradually whisk in the eggs, adding 1 tbsp of the flour mixture halfway through to prevent the mixture from curdling. Fold in the remaining flour mixture, almond extract, orange zest and juice.

Divide the batter between the prepared tins and bake in the preheated oven for 20–25 minutes, or until firm to the touch, or a skewer comes out clean. Leave in the tins for a minute or two, then turn the cakes out on to a wire rack. Remove the papers and leave until cold.

When ready to serve, simply place one of the cakes upside down on to a serving plate or cake stand and spread the flat surface with the crème fraîche. Spread the flat surface of the second cake with the apricot jam and sandwich the two together. Sift over a dusting of icing sugar and decorate with the pansies.

rippled chocolate meringue nest

A soft marshmallowy cloud of rippled meringue filled with a chocolatey cream and piled high with Easter eggs. The unfilled meringue can be made two days ahead and stored in an airtight container.

Serves 8–10

FOR THE MERINGUE

100g 60–70% cocoa solids
    chocolate, chopped

3 tsp cornflour

2 tsp white wine vinegar

1 tsp vanilla extract

5 egg whites, at room
    temperature

pinch of salt

250g white caster sugar

FOR THE FILLING

200g 60–70% cocoa solids
    chocolate, finely chopped

300ml double cream

1 tbsp golden syrup

FOR THE DECORATIONS

40g 60–70% cocoa solids
    chocolate, finely chopped

Matchmakers chocolates

sugar-coated chocolate eggs

chocolate birds (optional)

Preheat the oven to 140°C/fan 120°C/275°F/gas mark 1. Line one large or two smaller baking trays with baking parchment and, using a 20cm round plate, draw two circles (make sure they're spaced apart if using one tray). Turn the parchment over.

Melt the chocolate in a heatproof bowl set over simmering water. (Do not allow the bowl to touch the water.) Cool. Meanwhile, in a small bowl, mix the cornflour, vinegar and vanilla. In a large, clean bowl, using a food mixer or a hand-held electric whisk, whisk the egg whites and salt to soft peaks. Continue to whisk, adding the sugar a spoonful at a time, alternating with the cornflour mixture. It will be thick and marshmallowy. Stick the baking parchment to the baking tray or trays with blobs of the mixture, to stop it moving around. With a large metal spoon, fold the melted chocolate in roughly, for a rippled meringue.

Spoon the meringue between the circles on the baking parchment, spreading it to the edge of each. Raise the outside edge of one of the meringues and make a slight indent in the centre. Bake for one hour. Turn off the oven and leave the meringues to cool down completely inside. Don't open the door. They will be crisp and a bit cracked, with marshmallowy centres.

For the filling, place the chocolate in a bowl. Bring the cream just to a boil, pour over the chocolate and stand for a few minutes. Stir until smooth, adding the syrup, then whip until thickened. Melt the 40g of chocolate for the decoration in a small bowl, or in a microwave. Using a fork, flick it over the meringues. Allow to set.

When ready to serve, dab chocolate cream into the centre of a cake stand or plate, place the meringue that isn't indented on top and spread with half the filling, to the edge. Add a few Matchmakers chocolates, to resemble a nest. Place the indented meringue on top. Spread the remaining chocolate cream in the centre and fill with Matchmakers, eggs and birds, if you like.

simnel cake

The perfect cake to celebrate Easter. This is a lighter spiced fruit cake than that we associate with Christmas, and the baked marzipan centre results in a deliciously moist, very moreish cake.

Serves 8

FOR THE MARZIPAN

200g ground almonds

140g icing sugar, plus more
   to dust

140g golden caster sugar

2 drops of almond extract

1 tsp lemon juice

1 egg, lightly beaten

FOR THE CAKE

220g unsalted butter, very soft,
   plus more for the tin

170g self-raising flour, sifted

1 tsp baking powder

1 tsp ground cinnamon

½ tsp freshly grated nutmeg

1 tsp ground ginger

50g ground almonds

220g light muscovado sugar

finely grated zest of 1 lemon

finely grated zest of 1 orange

4 eggs, lightly beaten

200g sultanas

70g currants

150g glacé cherries, halved

50g mixed peel, in chunks

TO FINISH

2 tbsp apricot jam (or honey)

1 egg yolk, beaten

freshly picked and dry edible
   flowers, such as primroses

selection of 70cm lengths of
   4–5mm-wide ribbon

For the marzipan, put the ground almonds and sugars into a bowl. Add the almond extract, lemon juice and enough egg to bind. Knead only lightly. Remove one-third, roll out on a work top dusted with icing sugar and cut out a 20cm circle. (Seal the remainder in a plastic food bag until needed.)

Preheat the oven to 160°C/fan 140°C/325°F/gas mark 3. Butter a 20cm round, deep cake tin and line with baking parchment. Fold a strip of brown paper around the outside and tie with string.

Sift the flour, baking powder and spices into a bowl and add the ground almonds. Place the butter, sugar and zests into the bowl of a food mixer. Cream until light and fluffy, then add the egg slowly, with 1 tbsp of the flour mixture halfway through to prevent curdling. Add the remaining flour mixture a little at a time, alternating with the dried fruits, glacé cherries and peel.

Spread half the batter into the tin and add the circle of marzipan. Spoon over the remaining batter, smooth and bake for 1¾–2 hours, or until well risen and a deeper brown. (If necessary, lay a piece of foil with a hole over the top to stop it over-browning.) Leave in the tin for 15 minutes, then turn on to a rack to cool.

Use half the remaining marzipan and a work top dusted with icing sugar to roll out another 20cm circle. Warm the jam gently in a pan, then push it through a sieve (if using honey, simply warm it gently). Turn the cake over and brush the flat surface with most of the jam. Place the circle of marzipan on top, and make a criss-cross pattern on it with a knife. Use the side of a teaspoon or the back of a knife to scallop the edge. Roll 11 balls from the remaining marzipan, and stick them on with the remaining jam.

Glaze with egg yolk, and place under a hot grill (watch like a hawk), or use a kitchen blowtorch, until it is a lightly toasted gold. Decorate with the flowers and ribbons just before serving.

easter rabbit biscuits

Makes 14

120g unsalted butter, softened

80g golden caster sugar, plus
   more to sprinkle

1 egg, separated

200g plain flour, plus more
   to dust

1 tsp ground cinnamon

½ tsp mixed spice

pinch of salt

80g currants

1 tbsp whole milk

TOOLS

10cm rabbit cutter, or other
   cutter of your choice

As a child I always looked forward to Easter. We had exquisitely decorated chocolate eggs or rabbits on the breakfast table, an Easter egg hunt in the garden and, after eating all that chocolate, these Easter biscuits for tea. Here is the recipe my mother used; her biscuits were round with a fluted edge. I like these rabbit shapes, but use any cutter of your choice.

Line two baking trays with baking parchment. Using a food mixer, a large bowl and a hand-held electric whisk, or a large bowl and a wooden spoon, cream the butter and sugar together and beat in the egg yolk. Sift in the flour, spices and salt. Stir in the currants and milk to make a pliable dough. Do not over-mix, or you will toughen the biscuits. Wrap in cling film and chill for 30 minutes. Preheat the oven to 190°C/fan 170°C/375°F/gas mark 5.

Lightly flour a work top and a rolling pin and roll the dough out to 5–6mm thick. Cut biscuits out quite close together. You need to press down hard to cut through the currants! Re-roll the dough and cut out the biscuits until all the dough is used. At this point, you can freeze the cut-out biscuits. Place on the baking trays and bake in the preheated oven for about 10 minutes.

Remove from the oven, brush each biscuit with a very little of the egg white and sprinkle with a little caster sugar. Return to the oven for five to seven minutes, until golden. If you've used a smaller cutter, bear in mind that the baking time will be slightly less than for my 10cm-long rabbits, so keep an eye on them.

Leave on the tray for a few minutes to harden a bit, then carefully remove to cool on a wire rack. These will keep well in an airtight container for a few days.

little chocolate egg nests

These are filled with a caramel centre and topped with tiny eggs. Two things to be aware of: make sure the butter is soft, and use a large star nozzle, or it will be impossible to pipe the mixture.

Makes 20

250g unsalted butter, really soft

60g icing sugar, sifted

200g plain flour, sifted

20g cocoa, sifted

75g cornflour, sifted

FOR THE FILLING

6 tbsp dulce de leche or
    caramel spread

pot of chocolate sprinkles

60 sugar-coated chocolate eggs

TOOLS

large piping bag fitted with
    a large star nozzle

Line two baking trays with baking parchment.

Cream the butter and icing sugar until light and fluffy. Stir in the flour, cocoa and cornflour until just mixed. Spoon into the piping bag. Pipe 20 nests on to the prepared trays. Leave to rest in the fridge for 30 minutes. Preheat the oven to 190°C/fan 170°C/375°F/gas mark 5. Bake the little nests in the preheated oven for 12–15 minutes, then cool on the trays. These will keep, unfilled, in an airtight tin for a few days.

Using a teaspoon, place a little dulce de leche into the centre of each nest, decorate with sprinkles and top with three of the sugar-coated eggs.

viennese whirls

A variation of the above, these are one of the first things I baked as a child, and I still love them.

Makes 20, or 10 'sandwiches'

250g unsalted butter, really soft

60g icing sugar, sifted

1 tsp vanilla extract

220g plain flour, sifted

75g cornflour, sifted

FOR THE BUTTERCREAM

125g unsalted butter, really soft

200g icing sugar, sifted

2 tbsp milk

1 tsp vanilla extract

a little raspberry jam

Make the biscuits as above, creaming the butter and sugar with the vanilla. Pipe, chill, bake and cool as above.

To make the buttercream, cream the butter using a food mixer, or a bowl and a hand-held electric whisk, then add about half the icing sugar, the milk and vanilla. Beat until light and fluffy, then add the remaining icing sugar.

When the Viennese whirls are cold, spread buttercream on the flat surface of half of them with a small palette knife. Top with raspberry jam and place another whirl on top, to make 'sandwiches'. Dust with icing sugar.

sticky lime and coconut loaf with malibu cream

The sharpness of the lime combines with the creamy mellow coconut in this delicious cake, and will excite even the most jaded palates. This cake is extra moist as it is laced with a lime syrup and you may think, as you pour it over the freshly baked cake, that you have made too much. Have faith, for that is this cake's most delicious secret! I think the creamy topping makes the cake extra special, but it could be omitted or served separately.

Serves 8

FOR THE CAKE

175g unsalted butter, very soft, plus more for the tin

175g self-raising flour, sifted

1 tsp baking powder

175g golden caster sugar

3 eggs, lightly beaten

finely grated zest and juice of 1 lime (organic if possible), plus finely grated zest of 1 lime to serve

80g grated, creamed coconut (from a block), or desiccated coconut

FOR THE SYRUP

finely grated zest and juice of 2 limes (organic if possible)

120g golden caster sugar

FOR THE MALIBU CREAM

100g mascarpone

100g crème fraîche

20–30g golden caster sugar

2 tbsp Malibu (optional)

coconut, preferably freshly grated, or flaked, toasted or desiccated (optional)

Preheat the oven to 180°C/fan 160°C/350°F/gas mark 4. Butter a 900g loaf tin and line the base with baking parchment.

I use my food mixer and beater attachment, but you could use a bowl with a hand-held electric whisk or a food processor. This is a very easy, fail-proof method. First, sift the flour and baking powder into the bowl. Add the sugar, butter (in pieces) and eggs. Beat, but don't over-mix, then add the lime zest and juice and the coconut. Mix gently, scrape into the tin and bake in the preheated oven for 35–40 minutes. It is ready when it springs back to the touch, or a skewer comes out clean.

Meanwhile, make the lime syrup: simply mix the lime zest, juice and sugar in a bowl. As soon as the cake comes from the oven, prick it all over with a cocktail stick and, while it is still in the tin, evenly pour on the syrup. Leave to cool completely in the tin.

When ready to serve, place on a serving dish. Mix the mascarpone in a bowl until it is softened and add the crème fraîche, caster sugar and Malibu, if using. Spread over the cake and sprinkle with coconut, if using, and the lime zest.

blood orange, lemon and almond cake

I couldn't resist including a version of this classic orange and almond cake, originally from Syria and popularised by Claudia Roden. It is dead simple to make and the perfect accompaniment to Spring Rhubarb Compote (see page 15), or Pomegranate Jewels in Syrup (see page 22); drain them both well before using, and add a dollop of crème fraîche to the plate too.

I've used a blood orange here with a lemon, but any combination of sweet oranges – navel or clementines – could be used. Just make sure the total weight of citrus is 300–350g.

Serves 8

FOR THE CAKE

1 large blood orange (organic
  if possible)
1 unwaxed lemon
unsalted butter, for the tin
plain flour, for the tin
6 eggs
220g golden caster sugar
250g ground almonds
1 tsp baking powder
½ tsp salt

FOR THE CANDIED ORANGES

50g caster sugar
1 blood orange (organic if
  possible), thinly sliced

FOR THE GLAZE

4 tbsp marmalade, warmed and
  pushed through a sieve

Place the whole, washed unpeeled orange and lemon into a pan and cover with water. Bring to a boil, then reduce the heat and simmer for two hours, or until completely soft. (Top up the water every now and then.) Drain and cool. Remove the top stalk ends, cut both fruits in half and remove the seeds. Blitz in a food processor to a purée. (Alternatively, you can prick the fruit all over and microwave for eight to 10 minutes, until completely soft.)

Preheat the oven to 190°C/fan 170°C/375°F/gas mark 5. Lightly butter a 30 x 10 x 10cm loaf tin, (or a 20cm round, 7.5cm deep cake tin) and line the base with baking parchment. Dust with the flour, turning to coat, then tap out the excess.

Whisk the eggs and sugar for a minute or so in a large mixing bowl, then fold in the ground almonds, baking powder, salt and orange and lemon purée. Pour into the prepared tin and bake for 50 minutes to one hour, or until a skewer comes out clean. (You may need to cover the edges with foil for the last 15 minutes if the surface is becoming too dark.) The cake should be a beautiful golden colour. Leave to cool completely in the tin.

Meanwhile, make the candied oranges. Place 50ml of water into a small pan with the sugar and place over a low heat until the sugar dissolves. Increase the heat to medium and add the orange slices. Simmer for 10–15 minutes, until softened. Remove with a slotted spoon and cool on a wire rack lined with baking parchment, to stop the slices from sticking. Place the cake on a wire rack, brush all over with the marmalade and arrange the orange slices on top.

spring celebration cake: blossoms and butterflies

A beautiful two-tiered cake. All the decorations can be made ahead and stored in cardboard boxes (even for a couple of months). The un-iced cakes can be baked and frozen a couple of weeks ahead. Once the cake is iced, it will keep in cool conditions for up to a week before its big day. But never chill a cake covered with sugarpaste, or sugarpaste decorations, or keep them in airtight containers, as the sugarpaste will 'sweat'. I have used quite a few cutters on this cake, but if you don't own them and don't want the outlay, simply decorate the cake with roses (no tools required, see page 63). Use this recipe more as an idea and create your very own floral masterpiece!

Serves 25–30 (small pieces)

FOR THE CAKES

butter, for the tins

1 x Lemon Madeira cake batter
  (see page 41)

FOR THE BUTTERCREAM

300g unsalted butter, softened

300g icing sugar, sifted

finely grated zest of 2 unwaxed
  lemons, and juice of ½–1

TOOLS

10cm diameter, 7cm deep round
  cake tin

15cm diameter, 7cm deep round
  cake tin

10cm round cake drum

2 x 20cm round or square thin
  cake boards

15cm round cake drum

25cm round cake drum

Preheat the oven to 180°C/fan 160°C/350°F/gas mark 4. Prepare the two tins, buttering both and lining the bases with baking parchment. Make collars with baking parchment for both. Divide the batter between the tins, ensuring they are the same depth. Bake the smaller cake for 35–40 minutes and the larger for 55–60 minutes. If the top surfaces brown too quickly before the cakes are fully baked, make circles of foil with holes in the centre and place over the cakes to protect the edges. Rest in the tins for a minute or two, then remove and cool on a wire rack. With a serrated knife, trim the tops so they are the same height.

To make the buttercream, using a hand-held electric whisk, beat the butter, icing sugar and lemon zest for about five minutes, until light and fluffy. Gradually add the lemon juice, continuing to whisk as you do so (you may not need all of it; taste as you go).

Turn both cakes upside down so the flat bases become the tops. Slice each cake twice horizontally so each has three layers. Sandwich some buttercream between the layers, keeping enough back to spread over the tops and sides of both cakes. Place the smaller cake on the 10cm cake drum, securing with a dab of buttercream, and lift on to a 20cm thin board. Repeat with the 15cm cake, securing it to the 15cm drum, and lift on to a 20cm thin board. Spread the remaining buttercream over the top and sides of both cakes.

250g white sugarpaste to make:

5 roses, 5 rose leaves, 5 daisies,
12 pink-edged white
blossoms, 12 primroses,
18 violets, 36 ivy leaves,
12 forget-me-nots and
6 butterflies

TO COLOUR THE SUGARPASTE
AND FLOWERS

I used Sugarflair food colour
pastes in the following
shades: Caramel/Ivory; Claret;
Primrose; Eucalyptus; Grape
Violet; Navy; Bitter Lemon/
Lime

TO COVER THE CAKES

1kg white sugarpaste, plus 1kg
white or cream sugarpaste for
the drum

icing sugar, to dust

1kg marzipan (for home-made,
see page 50)

TO COLOUR THE SUGARPASTE

For the flowers, blossoms and leaves, I used the following colours.
Do simplify if you prefer; I like mixing colours to achieve more
interesting subtle shades. To make a pale cream, add a little
Caramel/Ivory to the 250g of white sugarpaste: dip a cocktail
stick or fine skewer into the food colour paste and drag it across
the sugarpaste. Knead until it's an even colour and you achieve
the desired shade. I then use this cream as a base for all the other
colours, it means they are slightly muted and more interesting.
To make pink, add Claret; to make yellow, add Primrose; to make
green, add Eucalyptus; to make purple, add Grape Violet; to make
blue, add Navy and Grape Violet.

Colour the 1kg sugarpaste a soft green, using tiny amounts of
Caramel/Ivory first, then Eucalyptus and Bitter Lemon/Lime. Store
in a sealed polythene bag at room temperature until ready to use.

To colour the sugarpaste to cover the drum, either add a tiny
amount of Caramel/Ivory to white sugarpaste, or use a ready-
made cream sugarpaste.

TO COVER THE BASE DRUM AND CAKES

Dust the 25cm round drum with icing sugar and sprinkle with
water. Knead the 1kg cream sugarpaste until pliable and roll out a
circle on a work top dusted with icing sugar, slightly larger than
the 25cm drum and about 4mm thick. Wrap loosely around your
rolling pin and lift on to the drum, smoothing with your hands.
Using a sharp knife, trim away the excess overhanging the edge.

If the buttercream covering the cakes has dried a little, use a
palette knife to re-spread it. Knead the marzipan. Take two-thirds
of it and, lightly dusting a work top with icing sugar, roll it out to
about 5mm thick. Lift it on to the large cake on its drum, smooth
all over and cut off excess around the base, covering the sides of
the drum. Cover the smaller cake in the same way. Leave overnight
to firm up, if possible.

Brush the marzipan on both cakes with a little cooled boiled
water. Take two-thirds of the pale green sugarpaste, roll out and
apply to the large cake, as with the marzipan. Smooth down by
rubbing gently with your hands. It is important not to stretch it
and remember it dries out quickly. Cut away any excess. Cover the
smaller cake in the same way. Leave the cakes overnight to firm up.

TO ASSEMBLE AND DECORATE

60g bag of white royal icing

4 dowelling sticks

1m x 8mm-wide cream ribbon

icing sugar, to dust

pot of pink sugar pearls (I used
   PME Blush Sugar Pearls)

small piece of fine netting

1m x 1.5cm-wide cream ribbon

double-sided sticky tape

TOOLS TO DECORATE

set of PME ivy plunger cutters
   (small and medium)

2.5cm PME rose leaf plunger
   cutter

1.5cm violet cutter

1.5cm primrose cutter

Jem tool no 9

set of blossom plunger cutters
   – 13mm, 10mm, 6mm (for
   blossoms and forget-me-nots)

fine paintbrush

2cm daisy cutter

2cm butterfly cutter

TO ASSEMBLE THE CAKES

Spread 1 tbsp or so of royal icing into the centre of the 25cm drum. Gently ease the large cake off its thin board and on to the centre of the drum, using a palette knife. Insert the four dowelling sticks into the cake – one in the middle and three spaced around it – but ensuring they will be covered by the top tier. Push down each stick until it hits the drum, and mark with a sharp craft knife about 1mm above the surface. Remove and snap each stick, discarding excess, and replace. Spread a little more royal icing into the centre and place the smaller cake on top. Attach lengths of 8mm-wide ribbon to the base of each cake with a little royal icing, at the back where the ends join.

FOR THE FIVE ROSES AND ROSEBUDS

Split open a polythene bag. Roll a ball of pink sugarpaste in your hands the size of a large cherry tomato, shape it into a cone, then indent it to form a cone on top of a base. Make six balls of sugarpaste (each will become a petal) and lay on one side of the bag. Fold over the bag and flatten one side of each ball using your finger until it is quite thin on one side. Peel back the polythene very carefully. Taking one petal at a time, with the thinnest part uppermost, wrap it completely around the cone. Repeat with the second, placing it centrally around the seam of the first, then repeat with the third. You now have a rosebud! Fold the remaining three petals around the rosebud, tweaking them as you go with your fingertips. With a small knife, cut away the base, using the offcuts for your next rose.

FOR THE IVY LEAVES AND ROSE LEAVES

Roll out the green sugarpaste to about 2mm thick on a board very lightly dusted with icing sugar. Stamp out with the ivy and rose leaf plunger cutters, pressing down well so the leaf pattern indents the sugarpaste. Lay out to dry, tweaking so they are not completely flat.

FOR THE VIOLETS

Roll out the purple sugarpaste to about 2mm thick and cut out using the violet cutter. Pipe a dot of royal icing in the centre of each.

FOR THE PRIMROSES

Roll out a cone in yellow sugarpaste and place, base down, on a work top. Using a cocktail stick, stroke the edges of the base outwards, thinning them to replicate how a petal tapers, then cut out a primrose with the cutter. Turn the cone over and press the Jem tool in to create the centre of the primrose.

FOR THE PINK-EDGED WHITE BLOSSOMS

Use the largest of the blossom cutters, and roll out white sugarpaste to about 2mm thick. Stamp out little blossoms. When dry, paint the edges with pale pink colour, formed by mixing Claret food colour paste with a little water. Place a sugar pearl in the centre, attached with a dot of royal icing.

FOR THE DAISIES

Roll out white sugarpaste to about 2mm thick. Using the daisy cutter, cut out daisies. To make the centres, roll out a tiny piece of yellow sugarpaste in your fingers and press down with a fine piece of netting to make a fine criss-cross pattern. Attach with a dot of royal icing.

FOR THE FORGET-ME-NOTS AND BUTTERFLIES

Roll out the blue sugarpaste to about 2mm thick and cut out blossoms (using the 10mm and 6mm blossom cutters). Pipe a dot of royal icing for a centre. Cut out blue butterflies, too, running a knife tip very lightly up the centre and bending the wings.

TO ATTACH THE DECORATIONS

Using the royal icing bag, attach the roses, leaves, blossoms and butterflies. I began at the top of the cake, placing the roses and rosebuds in the centre, then a few leaves and blossoms around.

Now decorate the base of each tier by creating a wreath of leaves and flowers around each cake. Finally, attach the 1.5cm-wide ribbon around the base drum, using double-sided sticky tape.

mini spring celebration cakes

These little cakes are to complement the larger Spring Celebration Cake (see pages 60–64), or they could be made as a display on their own. They would make a lovely gift for each guest at a special spring party to take home with them.

Makes 18

FOR THE CAKES

butter, for the tin

2 x batches of Lemon Madeira
    cake batter (see page 41)

4 tbsp apricot jam, warmed and
    pressed through a sieve

500g Lemon Buttercream
    (see page 61, made with
    250g each of butter and icing
    sugar, the zest of 1 lemon and
    juice of up to ½)

1kg marzipan

1kg sugarpaste, coloured as
    on page 62 (I made 250g pale
    green, 250g pink, 250g pale
    purple and 250g blue)

FOR THE DECORATIONS

60g bag of white royal icing

250g white sugarpaste, coloured
    and shaped into flowers, leaves
    and butterflies, as on pages
    62 and 64

TOOLS

20cm square cake tin

5cm round cutter

18 x 8cm thin round cake
    boards

18 x 20cm lengths of 1cm-wide
    ribbon, in a variety of pastels

Preheat the oven to 180°C/fan 160°C/350°F/gas mark 4. Butter the square cake tin and line the base with baking parchment. Make two batches of Lemon Madeira cake batter (see page 41), one at a time, and pour the first batch of batter into the tin. Bake in the preheated oven for about one hour. Repeat to make the rest of the batter and bake the remaining cake. When both are cold, cut each cake into nine rounds, using the 5cm round cutter. Trim the tops flat.

Lay out the 18 little boards and brush apricot jam into the centre of each. Place a cake, flat base-side up, on each board.

Using a palette knife, spread Lemon Buttercream over the top and sides of the cakes. Place them in the fridge to chill for 30 minutes; this results in a better-shaped cake that is far easier to cover. Roll out small pieces of the marzipan and coloured sugarpastes and cover the cakes, as with the large cake (see page 62).

Attach a length of ribbon to each cake, using the bag of royal icing to stick it once only where it joins. Decorate the little cakes differently as you please, using royal icing to adhere the blossoms, roses, leaves and butterflies as for the large cake (see page 64).

As with all cakes covered with sugarpaste, or with any sugarpaste decorations, do not keep them in the fridge or in airtight containers, or they will 'sweat'. They will keep well in cardboard boxes in a dark, cool place.

summer

summer cakes
hand-painted roses and crystallised flowers

We eagerly await our long summer (and hopefully sunny) days. Now is the time, despite the unpredictable British weather, when we can turn to easy outdoor entertaining. The abundance of glorious seasonal berries, fruits and flowers mean baking has never been so easy, and we don't want to spend long hours indoors when we have riches outside: sharp gooseberries, hedgerows filled with heady elderflowers, punnets of ripe strawberries and raspberries and heavy rose blooms in the garden.

Many of the recipes here rely on summer berries. It is hard to beat a Classic Victoria Sandwich filled with sweet strawberries and cream, or a pile of Little Blackcurrant and Almond Buns with a jug of home-made Muscatel Cordial. But stay on your toes: some of the best summer treats appear so fleetingly that you can miss them if you aren't careful.

I cannot wait for the arrival of Indian Alphonso mangoes in late spring and early summer. You will find the boxes stacked high outside Indian stores. Scatter the mangoes on pavlova, or bake them in puff pastry.

Capture the essence of summer in a jar and make Easy Strawberry and Elderflower Jam, or a floral sugar or two. They will enhance your baking even when the long days are over once more.

classic victoria sandwich

Almost nothing surpasses a freshly baked Victoria sandwich. Serve it up while lazing in the garden on a warm summer's day with a pot of tea. It is utterly delicious and completely foolproof to make with this all-in-one method. Really fantastic fresh eggs from my friend Sarah have made the cake in this photo a beautiful glowing yellow colour.

Less classic fillings can also be marvellous. Try sliced fresh strawberries instead of jam, or, for a lighter, simpler cake, just jam with no cream. Or try 2 tbsp lemon curd and a crushed meringue folded into 200ml lightly whipped cream, or swap the curd with dulce de leche for a caramel filling.

Serves 8

FOR THE CAKE

225g unsalted butter, really soft, in pieces, plus more for the tins

225g self-raising flour

1 tsp baking powder

4 eggs, lightly beaten

1 tsp vanilla extract (or seeds from 1 vanilla pod)

225g golden caster sugar

FOR THE FILLING

220ml tub clotted cream or double cream, lightly whipped to thicken

8 tbsp best-quality strawberry, raspberry or cherry jam, or Rose Petal Jelly (see page 108)

icing sugar, to dust

Preheat the oven to 190°C/fan 170°C/375°F/gas mark 5. Butter two 20cm round sandwich tins and line the bases with baking parchment. To make this all-in-one cake, you can use a food mixer, a large bowl and a hand-held electric whisk, or a food processor.

Sift the flour and baking powder into the bowl. Add the eggs, vanilla, sugar and butter. Cream together thoroughly, but not too enthusiastically as you want a light sponge. Divide the batter between the tins and smooth the surfaces.

Bake in the preheated oven for 25–30 minutes, or until a skewer comes out clean. Leave the cakes in their tins for a couple of minutes, then turn out on to a wire rack to cool. Leave until cold.

When ready to serve, select the best-looking cake for the top and place the other, baked top-side down, on a serving plate. Spread with cream. Spread the flat side of the top cake with the jam. Sandwich the two cakes together.

Dust with icing sugar and serve on the day it is made. The unfilled cake can be frozen ahead, but only fill it on the day it is served.

crystallising flowers

One of the easiest and prettiest ways to decorate any cake (or pudding) throughout the spring and summer. A wide selection of edible flowers and leaves can be crystallised, just do make sure they are dry and haven't been sprayed with insecticide.

In summer you can crystallise rose petals, rose buds, whole roses, pansies, mint leaves, sweet geranium leaves, daisies, lavender and anchusa. In spring, try pansies, primulas, primroses and violets.

1 egg white
white caster sugar
selection of dry edible flowers,
   petals or leaves
TOOLS
small paintbrush
fine florist's wire (optional)

Line a baking sheet or two with baking parchment. Place the egg white in a bowl and whisk it a little with a fork. Tip the caster sugar into another bowl.

Paint each flower, petal or leaf – one at a time – with egg white, being sure that every surface is lightly covered. Using a teaspoon, sprinkle over the sugar, holding the flower, petal or leaf over the sugar bowl, until every surface is covered. Gently shake off the excess and lay the flower, petal or leaf on a baking sheet.

If crystallising whole roses, either lay to dry on a baking sheet with the other flowers, or push a fine florist's wire through the base of the rose and hook the end of the wire over a glass. The flowers will dry hanging. Leave for 24 hours, or until thoroughly dry. The smaller petals and flowers will dry in a few hours, or overnight in a dry, warm place (an airing cupboard is perfect).

Store in a dry place in an airtight container. If they have been completely covered in egg white and sugar they may keep for many weeks, but any gap in the coating will shorten their lives.

summer extravaganza

Maximum impact with just a bit of effort and a wonderful centrepiece for any special occasion, even a small wedding. Everything on the cake is edible: crystallised roses, dog roses from the hedgerow, daisies, cherries and currants. For children, cover with sweets or biscuits. Just use your imagination!

Serves 30

FOR THE TOP TIER (15CM, SERVES 6);
MIDDLE TIER (20CM, SERVES 8);
BASE TIER (25CM, SERVES 16)

175g (225g; 550g) unsalted
   butter, really soft, in pieces,
   plus more for the tins

175g (225g; 550g) self-raising
   flour

1 tsp (1; 2) baking powder

3 eggs (4; 8), lightly beaten

1 tsp (1; 2) vanilla extract (or
   seeds of ½/ ½/ 1 vanilla pod)

175g (225g; 550g) golden caster
   sugar

FOR THE FILLING

100ml (200ml; 300ml) clotted
   cream, whipped

4 tbsp (8; 8) jam of your choice,
   plus more to stick

icing sugar, to dust

FOR THE DECORATION

crystallised flowers (see page 74)

200g cherries with stalks

150g redcurrants with stalks

TO ASSEMBLE

3 round thin cakes boards:
   15cm; 20cm; 25cm

8 dowelling sticks

30cm cake stand or serving plate

Follow the instructions for Classic Victoria Sandwich (see page 72), filling, in turn, a 15cm deep round cake tin, two 20cm sandwich tins and two 25cm sandwich tins with the batter. It's best to make the batter and bake the cakes one batch at a time. The batter in the 15cm tin needs to be twice as deep as that in the other tins. Bake the 15cm cake for 50–55 minutes (because it is very deep), the 20cm cake for 25–30 minutes, and the 25cm cake for 30–35 minutes. Cool, turn all the cakes upside down and fill (see page 72), cutting the small cake in half horizontally to do so.

Attach each cake to the right-sized cake board with a blob of jam. Check they are all level and, if not, trim them level with a serrated knife. At this stage they can be stored in the fridge for quite a number of hours, ready to be assembled a few hours before required. Dust all three cakes with icing sugar.

Insert four dowelling sticks vertically into the largest cake, spacing them apart to form a square sitting just within where the middle cake will rest. Push each stick down on the board until it will go no further, then mark with a pen about 1mm above the surface. Remove each stick, score where it is marked with a knife and snap. Replace the sticks into the holes. Repeat for the middle tier.

To stack the three cakes, simply place the largest cake, still on its board, on to a cake stand or serving plate. Place the middle tier on top, checking it is exactly in the centre, then add the top tier.

Now the cake is all ready for decorating. And this couldn't be simpler. Once you have crystallised your flowers (see page 74), simply arrange them on the cake with the cherries and currants. (A few carefully placed cocktail sticks can be useful to drape the fruit from.) You will have to decorate the cake on site, as it cannot be moved once the flowers and fruits have been arranged.

caramel meringue baskets with wild strawberries

Crisp on the outside and marshmallowy in the centre, pile these with any summer berries you have to hand and serve at a party. I have a few wild strawberry plants growing happily near the back door, producing tiny sweet berries all summer long and into the early autumn. Remember everything must be very clean and grease-free when making meringues, so firstly clean and dry your bowl and whisk.

Makes 12

FOR THE MERINGUES

3 egg whites, at room
   temperature

60g golden caster sugar

100g light muscovado sugar

FOR THE FILLING

300ml whipping cream, crème
   fraîche or double cream

icing sugar, to sweeten and to
   dust (or use Vanilla Sugar,
   see page 15)

1 tsp vanilla extract (or seeds
   from ½ vanilla pod)

300g wild or Alpine strawberries
   (or any other berries)

TOOLS (OPTIONAL)

large piping bag fitted with
   1.5cm star nozzle

Preheat the oven to 140°C/fan 120°C/275°F/gas mark 1. Line two baking sheets with baking parchment. Draw six 6cm circles (around a glass or little bowl), well spaced apart, on each tray. Turn the sheets of baking parchment over.

Place the egg whites in a scrupulously clean bowl and, using a hand-held electric whisk (or a food mixer), whisk until soft peaks form. Sprinkle in the caster sugar 1 tbsp at a time, whisking all the time, followed by about 2 tbsp of the muscovado sugar, again 1 tbsp at a time. It is important that the mixture is glossy, shiny and not over-mixed. Using a large clean metal spoon, fold in the remaining sugar; it is fine if it is rippled, just don't over-mix.

Now you can go two ways. Either spoon the meringue mixture into the piping bag, piping spirals and building the sides higher to contain the filling, or spoon the meringue on to the baking trays, making an indent in the middle of each (this will hold the cream and fruit later).

Bake in the preheated oven for 45–50 minutes, or until the outside is dry and crisp (the inside should still be a bit marshmallowy). Leave in the oven until cold. At this point, the meringues will store in an airtight tin for a couple of days.

Once the baskets are filled with cream and berries they soften, so assemble them just before serving. Lightly whip the cream and sweeten and flavour it with icing sugar and vanilla, or with Vanilla Sugar (omit the vanilla extract or seeds if using Vanilla Sugar). To serve, pipe or spoon each meringue full of cream and finish with berries. Dust with icing sugar, if you like, and serve.

best ever chocolate fudge cake

This recipe makes a great birthday cake, or a centrepiece for any celebration.

Serves 8–10

FOR THE CAKE

180g unsalted butter, really soft, in pieces, plus more for the tins

2 tbsp cocoa

100g 60–70% cocoa solids chocolate, finely chopped

150g natural yogurt

1 tsp vanilla extract

250g self-raising flour

1 tsp baking powder

1 tsp bicarbonate of soda

300g light muscovado sugar

3 eggs, lightly beaten

FOR THE FUDGE ICING

200g 60–70% cocoa solids chocolate, very finely chopped

300g double cream

1 tbsp golden syrup

Preheat the oven to 180°C/fan 160°C/350°F/gas mark 4 and butter two 20cm round sandwich tins, lining the sides with a 7cm-high collar of baking parchment (or use two deep tins if you have them).

Pour 200ml of boiling water over the cocoa and cool. In a heatproof bowl set over gently simmering water (make sure the bowl does not touch the water), melt the chocolate and stir in the yogurt and vanilla. When the cocoa mixture is lukewarm, add it to the melted chocolate, stir well and set aside. Sift together the flour, baking powder and bicarbonate of soda.

In the bowl of a food mixer (or in a bowl with a hand-held electric whisk), cream the butter and sugar for about five minutes, until really light. Slowly add the eggs with 1 tbsp of the flour mixture. Finally, gently fold in the flour and chocolate mixtures alternately with a large spoon.

Divide between the prepared tins and bake in the preheated oven for 30–35 minutes, or until a skewer comes out clean. Leave in the tins for a couple of minutes, then turn out to cool on a wire rack. Leave until cold.

To make the fudge icing, place the chocolate in a heatproof bowl. Bring the cream to the boil in a small pan and pour over the chocolate. Leave to stand for five minutes, then stir well and add the golden syrup. Once cool, whisk to thicken.

Use the fudge icing to sandwich the flat bases of both cakes together, spreading it with a palette knife. Spread the remaining icing over the top and sides of the cake.

sweetie and chocolate castle

I've made variations of this cake more times than I can remember. It is my most popular birthday cake ever, although to be honest, I have a feeling it could be more to do with the spectacular and alluring decoration than with the cake itself!

Serves 20

FOR THE CAKE

butter, for the tins

1½ quantities Best Ever
    Chocolate Fudge Cake
    batter (see page 80)

FOR THE BUTTERCREAM

150g 55–70% cocoa solids
    chocolate

225g unsalted butter, really soft

250g icing sugar

50g dark muscovado sugar

1 tsp vanilla extract

TO ASSEMBLE AND DECORATE

25cm square cake drum, or
    serving plate

3–5 mini chocolate Swiss rolls

3–5 thin wooden skewers

3–5 ice cream cones

3–5 paper or ribbon flags

selection of coloured sweets
    and chocolates

Preheat the oven to 180°C/fan 160°C/350°F/gas mark 4 and butter two 20cm square sandwich tins. Line the bases with baking parchment, lining the sides with a 7cm-high collar of baking parchment (or use two deep tins if you have them). Line one deep 15cm round cake tin in the same way.

Divide the batter between the prepared tins. It is important that the smaller cake is a bit deeper than the two larger cakes, which should be of an equal depth. Bake in the preheated oven for 35–40 minutes, or until a skewer comes out clean. Cool.

To make the buttercream, melt the chocolate over a heatproof bowl of gently simmering water, ensuring the bowl does not touch the water, then cool. Beat the butter until light and fluffy, then add the icing sugar, muscovado sugar and vanilla. Beat until really creamy. Pour in the melted chocolate and mix well.

Spread buttercream between the two larger cakes and sandwich together. Split the 15cm cake in half horizontally and spread buttercream between the halves. Turn all the cakes upside down, so you have flat tops. Spread buttercream all over both cakes. Dab a little buttercream into the centre of the drum or serving plate and place the large cake on to it. Centre the small cake on top.

Spread a thin layer of buttercream all over the Swiss rolls (you choose whether you want three or five turrets on your castle). Position each of them on to the top tier, and secure with a skewer into the cake. Place an ice-cream cone upside down on top, and add the flags. Decorate with the sweets and chocolates.

earl grey, cardamom and orange loaf

A very moist, light fruit cake to be cut thinly and maybe spread with a little butter. This is lovely with a cup of Earl Grey, or even jasmine or green tea, on a summer's afternoon.

Makes 12 slices

150g unsalted butter, in pieces, plus more for the tin

60g pecan nuts

15–20 cardamom pods

180g light muscovado sugar, or golden caster sugar

100ml Earl Grey or other tea, freshly brewed

260g mixed dried fruit (any you like, but I used 100g raisins, 100g sultanas and 60g currants)

200g self-raising flour

½ tsp salt

finely grated zest and juice of 1 organic orange

finely grated zest and juice of 1 unwaxed lemon

1 egg, lightly beaten

Preheat the oven to 180°C/fan 160°C/350°F/gas mark 4. Lightly butter a 30 x 10 x 10cm loaf tin and line the base with baking parchment. Place the nuts on a baking tray and cook for five minutes, or until toasted. Remove, cool slightly and chop.

De-seed the cardamom pods: split each with a knife, empty out all the little seeds and grind them to a powder in a mortar and pestle (discard the pod casings). Sift the powder to remove husks.

Put the butter, sugar, tea and dried fruit in a small saucepan. Bring to just below boiling point, then remove from the heat. Pour into a large bowl and cool to room temperature. Sift in the flour and salt and add the ground cardamom, orange and lemon zests and juices. Stir, add the egg, then the nuts. Mix until just combined.

Pour into the tin, smooth the surface and bake in the preheated oven for 50–55 minutes, or until a skewer comes out clean. Leave in the tin for a couple of minutes before turning out on to a wire rack to cool completely. This loaf stores well in an airtight container for a day or two.

cherry cola chocolate cupcakes

If the inclusion of cherry cola puts you off, do persist! These are very moist chocolatey cakes, with cherry jam both in the cake and the buttercream. If you don't want the bother of making chocolate cherries, simply decorate each cupcake with a fresh cherry instead.

Makes 12

FOR THE CUPCAKES

100g 60–70% cocoa solids chocolate, chopped

1 tbsp good-quality cocoa, sifted

200ml cherry cola

130g dark cherry jam

200g self-raising flour

1 tsp baking powder

½ tsp salt

150g unsalted butter, softened, in pieces

200g light muscovado sugar

2 eggs, lightly beaten

1 tsp vanilla extract

FOR THE CHOCOLATE CHERRIES

50g 60–70% cocoa solids chocolate, chopped

12 cherries, stalks intact

FOR THE BUTTERCREAM

200g unsalted butter, softened

300g icing sugar, sifted

1 tbsp milk

3 tbsp dark cherry jam

TOOLS

piping bag fitted with star nozzle

Preheat the oven to 190°C/fan 170°C/375°F/gas mark 5. Line a muffin tray (or trays) with 12 cupcake cases.

Place a heatproof bowl in a pan over gently simmering water and melt the chocolate with the cocoa and cola. Once all the chocolate has melted, gently stir in the jam and set aside to cool. Place another small heatproof bowl over the water and melt the 50g of chocolate for the cherries. Once melted, dip the cherries one at a time in the chocolate. Leave to dry on baking parchment.

Meanwhile, sift the flour, baking powder and salt into a large bowl and set aside.

In the bowl of a food processor, or in a large bowl using a hand-held electric whisk, cream together the butter and sugar until really light and creamy and paler; this will take about five minutes. Add the eggs and vanilla extract gradually, then fold in the sifted flour mixture. Finally, add the cooled chocolate mixture (the batter will be quite runny). Divide between the paper cases and bake in the preheated oven for 20–22 minutes. Leave in the tins for a couple of minutes, then cool on a wire rack.

To make the buttercream, place the butter and icing sugar in a food mixer and cream for about five minutes, until really fluffy. Add the milk. Warm the jam, press it through a sieve, then cool it. Gently mix into the buttercream; it will become a beautiful soft pink. Spoon into the piping bag and divide between the cupcakes. Top each with a chocolate-dipped cherry.

pigs' ears

I have been making these delicious biscuits for years now; I must have made many hundreds of trays! It's amazing, really, that just two ingredients can taste so good. The ear-shaped biscuits store well in an airtight container for a few days. They make a great accompaniment to summer fools, ice creams, or cups of tea. In summer, top them with whipped cream or sweetened mascarpone and summer berries (but only an hour before serving, or they will soften).

Makes 50–60

300–400g icing sugar, sifted,
    plus more to dust
380g shop-bought, all-butter
    puff pastry

You will need at least two non-stick baking trays (or bake in batches). Lightly dust a work top with icing sugar. Divide the pastry in two and roll one-half into a 2–3mm thick rectangle (roughly 32 x 23cm). Trim the edges and brush off excess icing sugar. Roll into a long, tight sausage. Repeat with the remaining pastry. Rest in the fridge to firm up for 10–20 minutes. Preheat the oven to 200°C/fan 180°C/400°F/gas mark 6.

Take one of the sausages and cut into rounds about 8mm thick. Sift a pile of icing sugar on a work top and lightly squash one of the spiral rounds of pastry on top of it, cut-side up. Dust a rolling pin with icing sugar and roll out to 1–2mm thick and a long oval shape, 8–10cm long. Lay on a baking tray and repeat until all the pastry is used up (or bake them in batches, which may be best in this case). You may need more icing sugar.

Bake in the preheated oven for 10–15 minutes in total, keeping a close eye on them as they turn from a beautiful caramel colour to burnt in no time. Believe me: I know from experience! After eight to 10 minutes, flip them over with a palette knife. Return to the oven until golden brown. Remove from the tray using a palette knife and cool on a wire rack.

gooseberry crumble cake with gooseberry and elderflower fool cream

Quite delicious, especially served warm, this brings together the classic combination of gooseberries and elderflowers. The two appear simultaneously, heralding the start of summer. Small gooseberries have the best flavour and the most tender skins. For a quick way to make the elderflower-scented gooseberry purée, mix in 3—4 tbsp elderflower cordial instead of infusing the elderflower heads.

Serves 8

FOR THE CAKE

125g unsalted butter, softened,
　plus more for the tin
120g small gooseberries, topped,
　tailed and halved
3 tbsp elderflower cordial, or
　to taste
100g golden caster sugar
2 eggs, lightly beaten
125g self-raising flour, sifted
½ tsp baking powder
½ tsp salt
finely grated zest of 1 lime
　(organic, if possible)

FOR THE CRUMBLE

130g plain flour, sifted
75g unsalted butter, chilled,
　in pieces
40g golden caster sugar

FOR THE FOOL

200g small gooseberries
4 tbsp golden caster sugar, plus
　more if needed
3 elderflower heads
200ml cold double cream
a little elderflower cordial
　(optional)

Preheat the oven to 180°C/fan 160°C/350°F/gas mark 4. Lightly butter a 20cm round springform tin and line the base and sides with baking parchment.

Place the gooseberries in a saucepan with the elderflower cordial and cook gently for a few minutes, until they soften a little. Strain and set the fruit and juice aside separately to cool.

To make the crumble, place the flour in a small bowl and add the butter. Lightly rub the butter into the flour with your fingertips to make a rough crumble mix, then stir in the sugar. Set aside.

Back to the cake. In a food mixer, or in a large bowl using a hand-held electric whisk, cream together the butter and sugar until light and fluffy. Add the eggs in stages, mixing between each addition; if it starts to curdle, add a spoonful of flour after each egg. Fold in the remaining flour, the baking powder and salt, then the gooseberries and lime zest, mixing gently. If it is very stiff, add a little of the strained gooseberry juice. Spoon into the tin and smooth the top. Sprinkle over the crumble, right to the edges, and bake for 30—35 minutes, or until a skewer comes out clean. Leave in the tin for five minutes, then turn out on to a wire rack to cool.

Meanwhile, make the fool. In a pan, place the gooseberries, 4 tbsp of water, the sugar and elderflower heads. Cook over a gentle heat until the berries soften. Push through a nylon sieve, then cool.

Whip the cream to soft peaks, then gently fold in the gooseberry purée. Add a little more sugar, or elderflower cordial, if required, cover and chill in the fridge until needed. Serve with the cake.

caramelised alphonso mango mojari

One of the simplest recipes in this book, this is also one of the most delicious; mojari is a Hindu word for slippers. Make this during the Alphonso mango season, in late spring and early summer. Serve with crème fraîche, or with lightly whipped cream flavoured with cardamom.

Interestingly, the paisley design we all know in fact originated in India, where it was based on the exquisite tear-drop mango shape.

Makes 8

4 ripe Alphonso mangoes,
   firm and not over-ripe
plain flour, to dust
300g all-butter puff pastry
about 40g unsalted butter,
   melted
about 60g golden caster sugar

Line two baking trays with baking parchment.

To prepare the mangoes, cut down either side of the central stones from top to bottom. Leave the flesh around the stone (keep it for later as it isn't needed here). As far as possible, trace the outline of a mango on to cardboard, then cut out to make a template. Carefully remove and discard the skin of each mango half. Set the fruit aside.

On a clean work top lightly dusted with flour, roll out the pastry to 2–3mm thick. Using your template as a guide (or one of the cut mangoes), cut out eight pastry cases, allowing 1–2cm more than the template all around the border. Prick the pastries with a fork, leaving the very edges. Lay on the baking trays and rest in the fridge to firm up for 20–30 minutes. Preheat the oven to 220°C/fan 200°C/425°F/gas mark 7.

When ready to assemble, thinly slice the mango halves, but not right through, then lift with a palette knife on to a pastry case. Brush generously with butter, then sprinkle generously with sugar.

Bake in the preheated oven for 15–20 minutes, or until the pastry sides have risen and caramel formed around the edges. It is important that it doesn't burn, or it will taste bitter. Each mango should have formed a delicious caramel over the top, and remain soft underneath.

Remove from the trays and cool on a wire rack. If you have made these ahead, crisp them up again by placing in a moderately hot oven for a few minutes to warm through.

mini elderflower almond cakes

In June, once the hedgerows and lanes are filled with tiny lacey elderflower flowers, it feels as though summer has finally arrived. For a summer party, you could also make lavender and rose cakes, using Lavender or Rose Sugar (see page 104) instead of caster and icing sugars. These cakes are butter- and flour-free.

Makes 8 individual cakes (or about 12 if using a cupcake tin)

FOR THE CAKES

70ml sunflower oil, plus more
    for the tin

2 eggs

1 tsp vanilla extract

2 tbsp elderflower cordial (omit
    for rose or lavender cakes)

finely grated zest of ½ lemon

125g ground almonds

25g fine semolina, or plain flour

1 tsp baking powder

80g golden caster sugar

FOR THE SYRUP (OPTIONAL)

juice of ½ lemon

50g golden caster sugar

1–2 tbsp elderflower cordial

2 elderflower heads

FOR THE DRIZZLE (OPTIONAL)

100g icing sugar, sifted

1–2 tsp elderflower cordial

3–4 tsp lemon juice

TO DECORATE

small sprigs of elderflower (or
    other flowers as appropriate)

Oil an eight-mould tray, or a 12-hole cupcake tray. (For the lovely photo overleaf, I used a fluted eight-mould canelé tray.) Preheat the oven to 180°C/fan 160°C/350°F/gas mark 4.

Crack the eggs into a bowl and beat in the vanilla, oil, elderflower cordial and lemon zest. In a large bowl, mix the ground almonds, semolina, baking powder and sugar. Tip in the egg mixture and mix everything together.

Divide between the moulds and bake in the preheated oven for 18–20 minutes (or 15–18 minutes for cupcakes), or until the centres spring back to the touch, or a skewer comes out clean.

Meanwhile, make the syrup by placing all the ingredients in a pan with 70ml of water and stirring. Bring slowly to a simmer and cook until it thickens to a syrup; this will take a few minutes. Allow the cakes to cool in the tins for a few minutes, then tap them out on to a wire rack. Place a large piece of baking parchment under the rack to catch the drips. Carefully spoon the syrup over the little cakes while they are still warm.

Alternatively, when the cakes are ready, remove from the tray on to a wire rack with a large piece of baking parchment underneath. When cold, make the drizzle. Place the icing sugar in a bowl and pour in enough elderflower cordial and lemon juice to make a slightly runny icing. Drizzle over the cakes in a random fashion. Decorate with a few sprigs of fresh elderflower (or other appropriate floral decorations).

muscatel cordial

We make this from the end of May and throughout June. This syrup is to my mind even more delicious than straight elderflower cordial, both to dilute with sparkling water or to drizzle in a chilled glass of prosecco. Constance Spry referred to it sprinkled over a bowl of strawberries as 'something quite out of the ordinary… an exquisite syrup with a flavour like muscatel'.

Makes about 1 litre
1kg golden caster sugar
1kg gooseberries, washed
   (no need to top or tail)
1 unwaxed lemon, sliced
12 elderflower heads, rinsed

Put the sugar and 600ml of water into a large pan and set over a gentle heat, stirring until the sugar dissolves. Increase the heat and bring to a simmer, adding the berries, lemon and elderflowers.

Simmer until the berries are softened, but not broken. Strain, cool, then bottle in dry sterilised bottles (see page 27) and store in the fridge, where it will keep for a few months. Once opened, keep it in the fridge; it should be fine for up to three months.

homemade lemonade

Makes about 400ml strong cordial
4 unwaxed lemons
caster sugar, to taste
sparkling water, to dilute

Remove the zest from the lemons with a vegetable peeler (do not include any white pith). Place in a small pan with water to cover (about 200ml) and simmer (do *not* boil) for a few minutes.

Meanwhile, squeeze the juice from the lemons and strain into a large jug. Strain the lemon zest-infused water into the jug and sweeten to taste (I used 7–8 tbsp sugar). The lemonade will be strong. Dilute with sparkling water and serve with floral ice cubes.

VARIATION: PINK LEMONADE
Add 2–3 tbsp raspberry sauce (see page 115).

FLORAL ICE CUBES
Use unsprayed edible flowers. Half-fill an ice cube tray with cooled boiled water. Place a rose bud, rose petal, or small flower into each indentation. (Daisies, violas and lavender sprigs also work.) Freeze. After an hour or two, top up with water and freeze.

peanut butter and sour cherry cookies

One of the best biscuit recipes I know to pack up and take on a picnic, as the salty peanut butter combined with the sweet cherries makes them a hit with all ages. Substitute the same amount of chocolate chips for the cherries, if you prefer.

Makes 18–20

100g unsalted butter, softened, in pieces, plus more for the trays (optional)

170g light muscovado sugar

200g crunchy peanut butter

1 egg, lightly beaten

200g plain flour

1 tsp bicarbonate of soda

½ tsp salt

1 tsp vanilla extract

100g dried sour cherries, roughly chopped

Preheat the oven to 180°C/fan 160°C/350°F/gas mark 4 and lightly butter two baking trays, or line with baking parchment.

Using a food mixer (or a large bowl and a hand-held electric whisk), whisk together the butter and sugar until light and fluffy. Beat in the peanut butter and egg. Sift in the flour, bicarbonate of soda and salt, then add the vanilla and cherries. Mix together (but do not over-mix), until just combined to a soft dough.

Using a tablespoon, divide the mixture between the baking trays and flatten each biscuit with the tines of a fork. The mixture will spread a little, so space them out well. Bake in the preheated oven for 10–12 minutes, or until just colouring around the edges. The cookies will continue to harden as they cool, so it is really important not to over-bake.

Leave on the trays for a few minutes, then transfer to a wire rack to cool completely. These will keep in an airtight container for a few days.

very berry white chocolate tray bake

This cake really needs to be eaten on the day it is made — it is packed full of berries, and so is deliciously moist — great for stashing away and taking on a picnic.

Makes 20 squares

225g unsalted butter, really soft, in pieces, plus more for the tin

225g self-raising flour, sifted

1 tsp baking powder

225g golden caster sugar

finely grated zest of 1 large unwaxed lemon

4 eggs, lightly beaten

200g white chocolate, finely chopped

250g blueberries (or raspberries, or a mixture)

Preheat the oven to 180°C/fan 160°C/350°F/gas mark 4. Lightly butter a 30 x 23cm tray bake tin and line the base with baking parchment.

Place the flour, baking powder, butter, sugar, lemon zest and eggs into the bowl of a food mixer or food processor, or use a large bowl and a hand-held electric whisk. Cream together thoroughly. Gently fold in half the chocolate and all the berries.

Turn into the prepared tray, level with a palette knife and bake for 35–40 minutes, until the cake is golden brown and springs back to the touch, or a skewer comes out clean. Leave to cool in the tin.

Meanwhile, melt the remaining chocolate in a small heatproof bowl set over a pan of barely simmering water (make sure the bowl does not touch the water). Drizzle it over the tray bake.

Once the chocolate has set, cut the cake into 20 squares.

raspberry almond thins

These are quite delicious biscuits for a posh summer picnic. The biscuits can be made and frozen, unbaked, in advance, but once filled need to be served within a couple of hours, or they will soften. They are great with a cup of tea, or to accompany fruits, fools and syllabubs all summer long.

If you don't want to make the pastry cream, use 250ml lightly whipped cream, mascarpone or crème fraîche instead, flavoured with the seeds from half a vanilla pod.

*Makes about 26 biscuits
(13 sandwiches)*

FOR THE ALMOND THINS

**30g blanched almonds (or
ground almonds)**

**70g caster sugar (or Rose Sugar,
see below)**

**110g unsalted butter, softened,
in pieces**

**150g plain flour, sifted, plus
more to dust**

FOR THE CRÈME PÂTISSIÈRE

**½ quantity Crème Pâtissière
(see page 12)**

FOR THE TOPPING

350g raspberries

**icing sugar (or Rose Icing
Sugar), to dust**

TOOLS

5.5cm round fluted cutter

Line two baking trays with baking parchment. Preheat the oven to 190°C/fan 170°C/375°F/gas mark 5. If using blanched almonds, scatter on a baking tray and roast for five minutes, or until light gold. Set aside to cool. Place the nuts and sugar in a food processor and blitz until fine (stop before it turns oily). Add the butter, blend, then add the flour. If using ground almonds, simply mix with the sugar, butter and flour.

Turn the dough on to a lightly floured board and roll out to about 3mm thick. Using the cutter, cut out the biscuits and place on the prepared trays. Re-roll the dough and continue until it has all been used. At this point, you can freeze the cut-out biscuits.

Bake for 12–15 minutes until just beginning to brown. Cool on the trays for a few minutes, then remove to a wire rack. When cold, store in an airtight tin. Make the pastry cream as on page 12.

Top half the biscuits with a spoonful of the pastry cream and six or so raspberries. Spoon on a little more pastry cream and sandwich another biscuit on top. Dust with icing sugar and serve.

ROSE OR LAVENDER ICING OR CASTER SUGARS
I always have jars of these. I find them invaluable in summer baking, and they keep for months. Use sparingly and to taste.

Pick a large handful of unsprayed, dry, scented rose petals (remove the white ends) or 12 lavender heads. Lay them on kitchen paper on a tray to dry out for a day. Place in a food processor with 550g of sifted icing sugar, or caster sugar. Blend until fine. Store for at least one week for the flavours to develop, then sift. Keep, in an airtight container in a dark, cool place.

simplest ever jam tarts

So easy, and quite delicious. Make these extra colourful by using different jams, whatever you have to hand. Strawberry jam is the classic, but try Rose Petal Jelly, Cherry Vanilla Jam (see pages 108– 109) or any other flavour, a lemon curd or even dulce de leche. Pack in a tin and take on a picnic.

Makes 12

150g unsalted butter, softened, in pieces

80g icing sugar, plus more to dust

finely grated zest of 1 large unwaxed lemon

1 tsp vanilla extract

150g self-raising flour, sifted

20g cornflour, sifted

12 tsp jam

Preheat the oven to 190°C/fan 170°C/375°F/gas mark 5 and line a fairy cake tray with 12 paper cases.

Cream together the butter, icing sugar, zest and vanilla for a few minutes, until really light and creamy, then add the flour and cornflour. Place a walnut-sized ball of mixture into each paper case and press the centre down to make a dip. Bake for 15 minutes, or until light pale gold. Set aside to cool.

Using a teaspoon, place 1 tsp jam (or other filling of your choice) into the centre of each. Sift over a dusting of icing sugar and set aside to firm up. These will keep in an airtight tin for a few days.

jams and jellies
easy strawberry and elderflower jam

Strawberry and elderflower – two of our classic summer flavours – go hand in hand (though this recipe works equally well without the elderflowers, if not available).

Makes about 3 x 340g jars

1kg whole small strawberries, gently rinsed, dried on kitchen paper and hulled

700g jam sugar

juice of 1 lemon

6 elderflower heads (tied in a piece of muslin)

Place the strawberries and sugar in a bowl, mix and set aside overnight. Tip into a preserving pan, add the lemon juice and flowers, and place over a very low heat until the sugar dissolves.

Now increase the heat and boil for 10–15 minutes until thickening, stirring all the time. Test for a set (see page 109) and, when the jam is ready, remove the muslin bag and any scum. Cool for 30 minutes then, while still warm, pour into warm, dry sterilised jars (see page 27). Once opened, store in the fridge.

rose petal jelly

Use with caution: this is highly flavoured and not to be spread with abandon on a slice of bread. Picking and brewing up the mountain of petals required to make this divine jelly reminded me of the slightly dubious rose brews I made as a young child. I used to add a bit of my mother's Miss Dior, pinched off her dressing table, and couldn't understand why she wasn't very impressed.

This jelly is a simplified version of a recipe my friend Chris has given me. Her rose petal jelly, which she makes every summer, is the very best. The 500g of rose petals it requires is a lot so, if they're not available, just halve the recipe. This makes a very intense, strongly flavoured topping for scones and cream, little jam tarts, or a Classic Victoria Sandwich (see page 72) filled with a buttercream or cream filling.

When cooking with roses, do ensure they are pesticide free and use only those that are highly scented; those with a strong perfume tend to have the best flavour. Nearly all the old-fashioned scented roses can be good; look for strongly coloured deep or purply red or pink blooms. A few of my favourites are: Roseraie de l'Hay, Hugh Dickson, Madame Isaac Pereire, The Apothecary's Rose, Kazanlik, Rosa Mundi, William Lobb, Guinée, Cardinal de Richelieu.

Makes about 2 x 340g jars

500g freshly picked scented rose petals (see recommendations above), ideally picked on a dry morning

700g granulated or caster sugar

juice of 2 lemons

1–2 tsp rose water, to taste (if needed)

After picking the rose petals, cut off and discard the end white parts, rinse the petals in plenty of water, drain and place in a preserving pan. Pour over 1 litre of boiling water and leave for one hour.

When ready to make the jelly, stir in the sugar and lemon juice. Bring to a boil, stirring well all the time to ensure the sugar has dissolved. Simmer for 30–40 minutes, or until it thickens and turns really syrupy. Remove from the heat and skim the scum from the surface. Test for a loose set (see right).

Let it cool a little at this point, then taste and see if you need to add the rose water. Push through a nylon sieve, then pour into two warm, dry sterilised jars (see page 27). Cover with waxed discs, seal and label. This will keep for a few months in the fridge.

cherry and vanilla jam

Makes about 3 x 300g jars
850g dark ripe cherries
   (750g stoned weight)
juice of 2 lemons
2 vanilla pods, split lengthways
450g jam sugar

TO TEST FOR A SET

Before you begin making jam, place a few saucers or small plates in the freezer. When you think the jam might have reached setting point, remove the pan from the heat (to avoid overcooking), drop a teaspoon of jam on to a cold saucer, and leave until cool. If the surface of the jam wrinkles when you push it with your finger, it is ready. (For a loose set, look for only a slight wrinkle.) If it does not wrinkle, return to the heat to boil for a few minutes longer, then test again, using a second cold saucer. Continue until you reach setting point.

Thoroughly wash and pick through the cherries, discarding any that are too soft or very over-ripe. Remove the stems, cut in half and remove the stones. Tie the stones into a muslin bag.

Place the cherries, the bag of stones, the lemon juice and vanilla pods in a preserving pan over a very, very low heat, simmering gently until the juices begin to run and the cherries become tender. Remove the muslin bag and add the sugar. Over a low heat, stir until all the sugar has dissolved.

Remove the vanilla pods, scrape out the seeds (use the point of a knife) and return them to the jam.

Increase the heat to boil briskly for five or 10 minutes and test the jam for a set (see left).

Pour into warm, dry sterilised jars (see page 27) while still warm. Cover the surface with waxed discs, seal and label. Stored in the fridge, it will keep well for a few months.

blackcurrant ripple white chocolate cheesecake

This is unbaked, but such a useful easy recipe for the summer that I include it here. Change the fruits seasonally: raspberries, blackberries and strawberries all work well, but in these cases you won't need all the caster sugar. I particularly like using blackcurrants, as their sharpness cuts through the sweet white chocolate.

Serves 8

100g unsalted butter, melted and
   cooled, plus more for the tin
250g digestive biscuits
300g good-quality white
   chocolate
250g mascarpone
50g icing sugar, sifted
300ml crème fraîche
200g blackcurrants
100g golden caster sugar

Butter the base and sides of a 23cm round loose-bottomed cake tin very well, ensuring the lip of the base is facing downwards (it will be tricky to remove the cheesecake otherwise).

Place the biscuits in a plastic food bag, seal and bash with a rolling pin to make fine crumbs. Place in a bowl and mix in the melted butter. Press into the tin firmly and chill in the fridge to firm – this will take at least one hour – or leave until you are ready.

To melt the chocolate, break it into small pieces and place in a heatproof bowl over a pan of barely simmering water. (Do not allow the bowl to touch the water.) Set aside to cool slightly.

Place the mascarpone and icing sugar in a large bowl and gently beat to loosen. Add the crème fraîche and cooled chocolate. Mix thoroughly and tip over the base. Spread to the edges and smooth the surface. Chill to set for several hours, or overnight.

To remove from the tin, warm a palette knife in boiling water, wipe dry and run it all the way round the tin to release the cheesecake. Place it on a serving plate.

The blackcurrant coulis can be made the day before too. Place the currants (removed from their stems) in a pan with the caster sugar and 1 tbsp of water. Simmer for a couple of minutes, blend until smooth, then press through a nylon sieve. (You will only need about one-third of this for the cheesecake.) Drizzle it over the cheesecake and ripple with a cocktail stick, or the point of a knife. Serve the rest in a small jug as an accompaniment.

lucky dip meringues

Each stripy meringue hides a secret… piled high they will be the talking point at any child's party.

Makes about 20

FOR THE MERINGUES

4 egg whites, at room
   temperature

½ tsp cream of tartar

115g white caster sugar, sifted

115g icing sugar, sifted

selection of food colour pastes
   I used (all Sugarflair):
   Primrose, Claret, Mint Green,
   Egg Yellow, Grape Violet

FOR THE SECRETS

selection of the following:
   jelly tots
   Smarties
   chocolate drops
   dried fruit and nut mix

TOOLS

nylon piping bag fitted with
   a 1.5cm nozzle

2 or 3 paintbrushes

Preheat the oven to 140°C/fan 120°C/275°F/gas mark 1 and line two baking trays with baking parchment.

Place the egg whites in a very clean grease-free bowl and use a food mixer with a whisk attachment, or a large bowl and a hand-held electric whisk. Start by whisking on a low speed, adding the cream of tartar when it becomes foamy. Next, increase the speed until the egg whites form peaks. Begin to add the caster sugar a large spoonful at a time, whisking constantly; the mixture will become stiff, glossy and firm. Using a large metal spoon, fold in the icing sugar in a couple of stages.

Arrange your selection of secrets – sweeties, chocolates or dried fruit and nuts – on the trays. Place about 10 groups on each tray, spaced fairly well apart (see photo, above left).

Open the piping bag so it is turned inside out and, using the paintbrushes, paint three or four lengths of neat (not diluted with water) food colour paste, running from the nozzle and stopping within a few inches of the top. You can paint with one or two contrasting colours if you like.

Now carefully spoon the meringue into the bag and pipe on top of each secret. Bake in the preheated oven for 40–45 minutes until crisp on the outside but still soft in the middle. Cool on the trays. These will keep in an airtight container for a few days.

peach melba gateau

The quest for perfectly ripe, sweet, juicy peaches is the trickiest part of this. Three components: the fat-free sponge, poached peaches and raspberry sauce can be made the day before.

Serves 6

FOR THE SPONGE

unsalted butter, for the tin

60g plain flour

pinch of salt

2 eggs

½ tsp vanilla extract

60g golden caster sugar

FOR THE PEACHES

500g golden caster sugar

1 vanilla pod (seeds removed
   and saved for the cream)

4–5 ripe, sweet peaches

FOR THE RASPBERRY SAUCE

200g raspberries

icing sugar, to taste

good squeeze of lemon juice,
   to taste

FOR THE VANILLA CREAM

300ml double cream

seeds from 1 vanilla pod
   (or 1 tsp vanilla extract)

icing sugar, to taste

Preheat the oven to 180°C/fan 160°C/350°F/gas mark 4. Butter a 23cm round cake tin and line with baking parchment. Sift the flour and salt together a couple of times and set aside.

Take the bowl of a food mixer and the whisk attachment and run under the hot tap. Dry thoroughly. Crack in the eggs, add the vanilla and sugar and whisk slowly, then increase to the highest speed. After four or five minutes, the mixture will be pale and mousse-like. Using the whisk, drizzle a little back on to the batter. If it leaves a trail (called the 'ribbon stage'), it is ready. Using a large metal spoon, fold in the flour gently. Pour into the tin and bake for 10–12 minutes, or until it springs back to the touch. Turn on to a wire rack covered with baking parchment. Leave to cool.

For the peaches, place the sugar, vanilla pod and 500ml of water in a pan. Cut a circle of baking parchment the size of the pan. Place the pan over a gentle heat and slowly bring to a boil, stirring so the sugar dissolves. Boil for a couple of minutes. Add the peaches, cover with the baking parchment and simmer gently until slightly softened. Lift out with a slotted spoon. Peel off the skins, halve each, cutting through the natural line, then pit them. Place on a plate lined with kitchen paper. Reserve the syrup.

To make the sauce, take all but a handful of raspberries and place in a food processor with 2 tbsp of icing sugar and the lemon juice. Blitz, press through a nylon sieve, then add a little more sugar or lemon juice to taste.

Place the cake on a serving plate, flat base up. Mix 2 tbsp peach syrup with 1 tbsp raspberry sauce and spoon over. Lightly whip the cream until billowing, adding the vanilla and icing sugar to taste. Pile on the cake and spread over the top. Slice the peaches, arrange on the cake and drizzle with raspberry sauce (serve the rest in a jug). Scatter over the reserved raspberries and serve.

ondhwa (spicy savoury cake)

I've been asked for this recipe more times than I can remember! Every Gujarati home has a version of this delicious spicy, sweet and sour savoury cake, a healthy, filling snack at any time.

My recipe is based on that of my sister-in-law Gita, a brilliant cook. She taught me how to make this many years ago. Serve slightly warm with mango chutney and a cup of tea or glass of milk.

I have used a vegetable called dudhi (a gourd available in Indian shops), but you can use carrots, courgettes, cabbage, spinach or potatoes, or a mixture. I have used ondhwa flour (again available in Indian shops) made from ground lentils and rice.

Makes 16 squares

FOR THE CAKE

325g raw vegetables (prepared weight); choose from grated dudhi; shredded cabbage with carrots; grated potatoes with onions; or courgettes

500g plain yogurt

250g ondhwa flour

1 tbsp golden caster sugar

3 tbsp finely grated root ginger

leaves from a bunch of coriander, finely chopped

1–2 small chillies, chopped

salt, to taste

juice of ½ lemon

1 tsp baking powder

30g sesame seeds

FOR THE TEMPERING

200ml sunflower oil, plus more for the tin

1½ tsp carom (or cumin) seeds

1½ tsp mustard seeds

1½ tsp fenugreek seeds

1½ tsp turmeric

pinch of asafoetida (optional)

Preheat the oven to 190°C/fan 170°C/375°F/gas mark 5. Oil a square 20cm tin very well indeed. Measure all the spices for the tempering together into a small bowl and set aside.

In a large bowl, mix together the vegetables, yogurt, ondhwa flour, sugar, ginger, coriander leaves, chillies, salt and lemon juice.

Now temper the spices: place the oil in a small saucepan and heat it. I test to see if it is hot enough by dropping in a couple of cumin seeds; if they sizzle the oil is ready. Throw in all the spices together, they will crackle and pop and release a wonderful smell. Remove from the heat after 10–15 seconds as you don't want the oil to burn the spices. Allow to cool down for five minutes or so.

Pour the spices into the bowl of vegetable mixture and, using a large spoon, mix everything well. I add 3–4 tbsp of cold water to very slightly thin the batter. Taste for salt. Lastly, stir in the baking powder and pour the batter into the prepared tin. Sprinkle with sesame seeds and bake in the preheated oven for 40–45 minutes.

The cake is ready when it has formed a golden crispy crust on the top and has firmed up. It does continue to cook once you remove it from the oven. Cool in the tray and then cut into squares.

tarte aux fraises french strawberry tart

At school I had a French exchange friend, Anne, who lived in Brittany on the coast. I remember holidays staying in her family's beautiful clifftop house overlooking the sea and Mont Saint-Michel.

Every evening the long dinner table would be laden with huge artichokes, snails, crabs, lobsters, langoustines… all a little wasted on me at the time. Occasionally, for dessert, Madame presented a beautiful tart from the local boulangerie. Neither Madame nor myself were particularly svelte, so she took it upon herself to deny the two of us a slice! This tart is in memory of those days. Feel free to substitute any seasonal fruit or berries, such as peaches, apricots or a mixture.

If you don't want to make a pastry cream, simply whip 500ml whipping cream to soft peaks, adding 1 tsp of vanilla extract and icing sugar to taste, and use this instead.

Serves 6

FOR THE CRÈME PÂTISSIÈRE

300ml whole milk

1 vanilla pod

4 egg yolks

100g golden caster sugar

50g plain flour

small knob of unsalted butter

100ml double cream

FOR THE RICH SWEET PASTRY

150g unsalted butter, softened,
 plus more for the tin

250g plain flour, sifted, plus
 more to dust

pinch of salt

30g ground almonds, sifted

80g icing sugar, sifted

1 egg, lightly beaten

½ tsp vanilla extract

FOR THE STRAWBERRIES

630g strawberries, halved

4 tbsp strawberry jam, warmed
 and pressed through a sieve

Make the crème pâtissière (see page 12), cover and chill. Butter a loose-based rectangular flan tin – mine is 30 x 20cm – or a 25cm round flan tin (you may need more strawberries for a round tin).

To make the pastry, sift the flour and salt into a bowl and stir in the almonds. In a bowl using a hand-held electric whisk, or using a food mixer, cream the butter and icing sugar until just mixed, then add the egg. Slowly add the flour and vanilla and, as soon as it comes together, stop. Wrap in cling film and chill for one hour.

On a lightly floured board, roll out the pastry to a rectangle or circle about 3mm thick. Lift it into the tin, pressing in gently. Remove excess pastry by running the rolling pin over the tin. Prick the base all over with a fork. Chill for about 30 minutes. Preheat the oven to 190°C/fan 170°C/375°F/gas mark 5 and put a baking tray in the oven to heat. Line the pastry case with baking parchment, fill with baking beans or raw rice, place on the hot baking tray and bake for 20 minutes. Remove the paper and beans and return to the oven for five minutes. Cool.

When ready to assemble (no more than a few hours in advance), remove the pastry from the tin and spread with crème pâtissière. Arrange the berries on top, brushing all over with jam for a shiny glaze. (If the jam's too thick, thin it down with 1 tbsp of water.)

sicilian lemon ricotta cake

Ideally eaten on a balmy summer's evening after a delicious dinner in Sicily! If that's not possible, then perhaps these delicious flavours will transport you to a past summer's holiday.

Serves 8

150g ricotta cheese

125g, plus 2 tbsp, pistachio nuts

100g unsalted butter, softened,
   in pieces, plus more for the tin

125g golden caster sugar

finely grated zest of 3 unwaxed
   lemons and juice of 1½

3 eggs, separated

2 tbsp plain flour, sifted

Put the ricotta in a bowl lined with muslin. Tie the muslin up with string to make a bag, then suspend the bag over the bowl in the fridge for a couple of hours, or overnight, until it has drained much of its liquid (the easiest way to do this is to secure the string to one of the fridge racks). Untie the bag, press the ricotta through a sieve and set aside.

Preheat the oven to 180°C/fan 160°C/350°F/gas mark 4. Put all the pistachio nuts on a baking tray and cook for five minutes, until toasted. Remove 2 tbsp, cool slightly, and roughly chop. Put all the rest in a food processor and grind to a powder (don't process them for too long, or they will turn oily).

Butter a 20cm, 7.5cm deep, round springform cake tin and line the base with baking parchment.

In a large bowl with a hand-held electric whisk, or in a food mixer, beat together the butter and all except 2 tbsp of the caster sugar, adding the lemon zest, until light and creamy. Add the egg yolks one at a time, beating between each addition. Tip in the ground pistachios and flour. Mix all the lemon juice into the ricotta, then fold it into the egg mixture.

In a scrupulously clean bowl, whisk the egg whites and add the remaining caster sugar. Fold into the cake batter and pour into the prepared tin. Sprinkle with the chopped pistachio nuts and bake in the preheated oven for about 40 minutes, or until a skewer comes out clean.

Cool in the tin on a wire rack, then carefully remove the tin.

little blackcurrant and almond buns

These little buns are not only child's play to make, but also transport me back to my childhood, when I could easily spend a whole summer's day picking blackcurrants in my parents' garden.

Makes 24

FOR THE CAKES

250g unsalted butter, really soft, in pieces

220g golden caster sugar

finely grated zest of 1 unwaxed lemon

4 eggs, lightly beaten

220g ground almonds

80g self-raising flour, sifted

200g fresh blackcurrants (or frozen and defrosted, reserving their juice), destalked, topped and tailed, plus a small handful to top the cakes

FOR THE ICING

200g icing sugar, sifted, plus more if needed

1 tsp fresh blackcurrant cordial (if using fresh currants in the cakes)

Preheat the oven to 180°C/fan 160°C/350°F/gas mark 4. Line two fairy cake tins with 24 paper cases.

Cream the butter, sugar and lemon zest until light and fluffy. Add the eggs very slowly then, using a large metal spoon, fold in the ground almonds, flour and blackcurrants. Divide the batter between the paper cases and bake in the preheated oven for 18–20 minutes, or until they spring back to the touch. Cool in the tins for a few minutes, then remove to cool completely on a wire rack.

To make the icing, place the icing sugar in a bowl and add the blackcurrant juice or fresh cordial with about 4 tsp of water, little by little, until you have a beautiful pink icing, neither too stiff nor runny. (Add more icing sugar if it is too runny.) Using a teaspoon, dollop a little on to each cake and top with a few blackcurrants.

honey cupcakes with lavender buttercream

These light floral cakes are quite delicious and are at their best if made on the day they are to be eaten. The meringue buttercream is lightly flavoured with lavender, making it a perfect recipe either for late summer or early autumn.

Makes 20

FOR THE CUPCAKES

300g plain flour

2 tsp baking powder

1 tsp ground cinnamon

½ tsp salt

225g unsalted butter, really soft

300ml runny floral honey

55g caster sugar, or Lavender
  Sugar (see page 104)

4 eggs, lightly beaten

finely grated zest of 1 unwaxed
  lemon, plus 2 tbsp of juice

FOR THE BUTTERCREAM

3 egg whites

170g caster sugar

240g unsalted butter, softened,
  in pieces

1 tsp lavender extract

finely grated zest of 1 large
  unwaxed lemon

TO DECORATE

50g granulated caster sugar

purple food colour paste

20 sprigs unsprayed lavender, or
  a sprinkling of dried lavender

TOOLS (OPTIONAL)

piping bag fitted with star nozzle

To make the coloured sugar for decorating, take the granulated sugar and mix in a little purple food colour paste with 1 tbsp of cold water. Spread the sugar on to a plate and, using your fingers, rub the colour into the sugar. Leave to dry for a few hours.

Preheat the oven to 180°C/fan 160°C/350°F/gas mark 4. Place 20 cupcake cases into two cupcake tins.

Sift together the flour, baking powder, cinnamon and salt. In the bowl of a food mixer, cream together the butter, honey and sugar until very light and fluffy (this will take a good five minutes). Gradually add the eggs, lemon zest and juice and 1 tbsp of the flour mixture. Gently fold in the remaining flour mixture. Spoon into the paper cases and bake for 18–20 minutes, or until the cakes spring back to the touch. Let cool on a wire rack.

To make the buttercream, place the egg whites and sugar in a pan and very gently warm up, stirring until the sugar dissolves. Pour the warm mixture into a bowl and whisk with a hand-held electric whisk until really stiff, glossy and doubled in volume; this may take five minutes. Continuing to whisk, add the butter 2 tbsp at a time. Stop as soon as the butter is mixed in. Mix in the lavender extract and lemon zest. If it becomes grainy, very gently reheat in the microwave and continue. The buttercream stores well in the fridge for a couple of days; whisk slightly before using.

Using the nozzle and piping bag, pipe the meringue buttercream on to the cakes (or spread it with a palette knife), sprinkle with the purple coloured sugar and add a sprig of lavender.

warm raspberry and coconut cake

Thank you to my dear friend Jacqui for sharing this wonderful recipe. It really is best of all served warm, I think, with a dollop of crème fraîche.

Serves 8

175g unsalted butter, really soft, in pieces, plus more for the tin

50g unsweetened desiccated coconut

175g golden caster sugar

175g self-raising flour, sifted

2 eggs, lightly beaten

3 tbsp canned coconut cream (freeze the remains of the can for another time)

150g raspberries

demerara sugar, for the top

Preheat the oven to 180°C/fan 160°C/350°F/gas mark 4. Butter a 23cm round springform tin and line the base and sides with baking parchment.

Put the desiccated coconut into a small pan, set it over a low heat and stir until it is a pale golden brown. Set aside to cool.

In the bowl of a food mixer, or in a large bowl using a hand-held electric whisk, or using a food processor, place all the ingredients except the raspberries and demerara sugar. Mix together only until it becomes an even cake batter.

Transfer to the prepared tin and scatter evenly with raspberries. Sprinkle with demerara sugar and bake in the preheated oven for 35–40 minutes, or until a skewer comes out clean. Cool in the tin on a wire rack for five minutes, then remove from the tin and cool slightly. Warm through slightly to serve.

strawberry lollipops

When I was very, very young, I remember listening out for the tinkling tune of the ice cream van and racing down the road with my brother for our Saturday afternoon treat. Mine was always a pale pink strawberry-flavoured milky cone (sadly no longer made). Here is my cake creation in memory of those childhood days. These are perfect for any child's summer party.

Makes about 24

FOR THE CAKES

60g unsalted butter, really soft, in pieces, plus more for the tin

100g self-raising flour

½ tsp baking powder

75g golden caster sugar

1 egg, lightly beaten

1 tsp vanilla extract

40–50ml whole milk, at room temperature

2 tbsp good strawberry jam

FOR THE ICING AND DECORATION

300g icing sugar

1 tbsp strawberry jam, warmed and pressed through a sieve

24 lollipop sticks (or candy canes)

multicoloured sprinkles

Preheat the oven to 180°C/fan 160°C/350°F/gas mark 4. Butter each hole of a 24-hole mini-muffin tin very well. (Or use a silicone mould and follow the manufacturer's instructions.)

Sift the flour and baking powder into the bowl of a food mixer, or use a bowl and a hand-held electric whisk. Add the butter, sugar, egg and vanilla and blend briefly, adding the milk slowly as you continue to mix. Gently fold in the strawberry jam (mash it with a fork to remove lumps first); it should be rippled.

Spoon the mixture between the holes in the prepared tin and bake in the preheated oven for 12–15 minutes, or until they spring back to the touch. Leave in the tin for a minute, then tap out on to a wire rack to cool.

Meanwhile, make the icing. Sift the icing sugar into a bowl and add cold water, little by little (I used about 3 tbsp). Then add the strawberry jam. The icing will be a pale pink, and quite thin.

Take a lollipop stick, dip one end into the icing and stick into the top of one of the little cakes. Repeat with all the lollipop sticks. Take a wire rack and support both short ends by sitting it over a deep tray lined with baking parchment to catch stray drips and sprinkles (I used a roasting tray). The wire rack should be elevated but stable.

Lay a sheet of baking parchment over the work top you will be working on. Holding them by the sticks, dip the cakes one at a time into the icing until more or less covered. When each has been iced, push its lollipop stick through a hole in the wire rack.

Sprinkle over the sprinkles while the icing is still wet. Leave to dry. These will keep in an airtight container for a day or two.

scented alphonso mango pavlova

To me the appearance of *Alphonso mangoes in the shops signals the arrival of the very earliest part of summer. During May in our house we devour this unrivalled fruit, with its creamy texture and heady perfume. They are simply delicious on their own (my husband believes there is no other way), but I've blended the Alphonso here with the flavours from one of my favourite yogurt dishes from Gujarat — saffron, cardamom and pistachio — to provide the filling for a marshmallowy meringue.*

You can get everything ready in advance earlier in the day (and the meringue a few days ahead), but assemble the pavlova only a couple of hours before serving.

Serves 8

FOR THE MERINGUE

3 tsp cornflour

2 tsp white wine vinegar

1 tsp vanilla extract

5 egg whites, at room
   temperature

pinch of salt

250g caster sugar

FOR THE FILLING

2 tbsp pistachios (or flaked
   almonds)

2 tsp milk

a few strands of saffron

20 cardamom pods

160ml whipping cream

400g plain yogurt

3 tbsp icing sugar, sifted

5 fully ripe Alphonso mangos

freshly picked dry, unsprayed
   edible flowers (optional)

Preheat the oven to 190°C/fan 170°C/375°F/gas mark 5. Scatter the pistachio nuts for the filling on a baking tray and roast lightly for three or four minutes. Cool slightly, chop and set aside. Reduce the oven temperature to 140°C/fan 120°C/275°F/gas mark 1. Line a baking tray with baking parchment and draw a circle on it (mine was about 24cm in diameter). Turn the paper over so the pencil mark is underneath.

To make the meringue, in a small bowl, mix the cornflour, vinegar and vanilla extract. In a very clean, dry, grease-free bowl, place the egg whites and salt. Using a food mixer or a bowl and a hand-held electric whisk, whisk until soft peaks form, then continue to whisk, adding the sugar a large spoon at a time, alternating with the cornflour mix. Spoon the meringue into the circle on the tray, hollowing the centre and building the sides higher. Bake for one hour, then turn the oven off, leaving the meringue inside until cold. You can store it now in an airtight container for a few days.

Warm the milk in a small pan and add the saffron. Set aside. With the point of a knife, split the husk of each cardamom pod and empty the seeds into a mortar. Grind to a powder, then sift to remove the husks. In a bowl, whip the cream to soft peaks and fold in the yogurt, cardamom, saffron milk and icing sugar.

When ready to serve, place the pavlova on a cake stand or plate. Spoon in the deliciously scented yogurt cream. Peel, then cube or slice the mangos and arrange on top. Scatter over the roasted pistachios. I also sprinkled it with alkanet flowers from my garden.

summer celebration cake: hand-painted cherries and roses

A lovely cake to make for a summer celebration or as a special edible gift. I've filled the cake with a delicious rose buttercream and a morello cherry jam to reflect the hand-painted decoration. You will need to allow the sugarpaste to dry overnight before painting. A simple scattering of petals would be lovely too, if sugarpaste and dabbling with a paintbrush is not for you!

The recipe here is an easy all-in-one yogurt cake that works well with the other flavours.

Serves 10

FOR THE CAKE

unsalted butter, for the tin

280g self-raising flour, sifted

1 tsp baking powder

200g golden caster sugar

250g plain yogurt

120g sunflower oil

3 eggs, lightly beaten

finely grated zest of 1 unwaxed lemon and juice of ½

1–2 tbsp milk, if needed

FOR THE BUTTERCREAM AND FILLING

130g unsalted butter, really soft, in pieces

280g icing sugar (or Rose Icing Sugar, see page 104)

1–2 tbsp milk

pink food colour paste

¼ tsp rose water (to taste; omit if you used Rose Icing Sugar)

3 tbsp dark morello cherry jam

Preheat the oven to 170°C/fan 150°C/340°F/gas mark 3½. Butter a 23cm springform tin well and line with baking parchment.

Sift the flour and baking powder into a bowl and stir in the caster sugar. In another large bowl, mix together the yogurt, oil, eggs and lemon zest and juice. Fold in the sifted flour mixture and, if the batter appears a little dry, add the milk.

Pour into the prepared tin and bake in the preheated oven for 35–40 minutes, or until a skewer comes out clean. Leave to cool in the tin for a couple of minutes, then transfer to a wire rack to cool down completely.

To make the buttercream, place the butter in a mixing bowl and whisk for a minute or so. Sift in the icing sugar or Rose Icing Sugar and whisk until really light and creamy. Add the milk and a pinprick of pink food colour (and rose water to taste if you did not use Rose Sugar; it will be overpoweringly floral otherwise!).

Turn the cake upside down and cut in half horizontally, so the flat base becomes the top. Spread pale pink buttercream over the cut surface (generously if not hand-painting the cake, but sparingly if you are). Spread with the cherry jam and place the other half of the cake on top. You now have a perfect, flat-topped cake. Sprinkle with pink rose petals if not proceeding with the further decorations and place on a cake stand or serving dish.

If you are making the hand-painted cake, cover the top and sides of the cake with buttercream.

icing sugar, to dust

2kg white sugarpaste

selection of food colour pastes,
   I used the following (all
   Sugarflair): Christmas Red,
   Claret, Christmas Green,
   Bitter Lemon, Party Green,
   Eucalyptus, Grape Violet

gum arabic powder

50g bag white royal icing

TOOLS

25cm round cake drum

30cm round cake drum

selection of paintbrushes

100cm 1.5cm-wide white satin
   ribbon

double-sided sticky tape

Place the cake on the 25cm round cake drum, sticking it with a little buttercream or jam. Lightly dust a work top with icing sugar. Knead half the sugarpaste until pliable and roll out to a circle about 5mm thick, and slightly larger than the diameter of the cake and sides. Lift with both hands (or roll loosely around the rolling pin) and place over the cake; the sugarpaste needs to cover both cake and drum. Smooth down gently, working quickly as it will dry out. Rub away any blemishes or creases and cut away the excess around the edges, keeping all the clean offcuts in a sealed polythene bag. To cover the 30cm cake drum, take the remaining sugarpaste and knead until pliable. Sprinkle a very little water over the drum and lightly dust with icing sugar. Roll out the sugarpaste and cover the drum in the same way as you did the cake, cutting away excess and storing clean offcuts as before. Leave both cake and drum overnight at room temperature to dry out.

Colour a very small piece of leftover sugarpaste (enough to make six red cherries) using Christmas Red and Claret food colours (see page 62). Roll into six cherry shapes. Colour another small piece using Christmas Green and Bitter Lemon food colours to make six cherry leaves. Roll out a tiny piece of green sugarpaste on a work top dusted with icing sugar and cut out leaf shapes using a small knife. Leave to dry overnight. Mix a little gum arabic powder to a paste with water and, using a small paintbrush, use it to put a shine on the cherries.

Next day, attach the ribbon to the drum with the double-sided tape. Place a dab of buttercream or a little jam in the centre of the drum. Carefully place the cake in the centre of the iced board.

It is best to work out your design on paper before starting to paint. After you have done so, paint directly on to the cake. It is best to do this gradually, just as in a watercolour painting. Should you wish to change something, it is possible by going over it with a clean, slightly damp paintbrush, letting it dry, then painting over. This cannot be done too many times in the same place as you are painting on sugar. I prefer fairly random designs anyway; that way you can change it as you go. Stick a few sugar cherries and leaves around the cake and drum using the royal icing.

This stores well at room temperature in a box for a few days (not an airtight container, or the fridge, or the sugarpaste will 'sweat').

autumn

autumn cakes
blackberries, cobnuts and marzipan acorns

Gradually the nights begin to draw in. For children and parents it is the end of the long summer holidays, but there is a back-to-school feel in the air for all of us. I love autumn: the golden mellow light, the glorious colours and the rustle of fallen leaves. The trees are laden with ripe apples, pears, plums and even figs, while blackberries fill the hedgerows. At this time of year I long to spend a few hours in the warmth of the kitchen, baking with gentle spices, cooking caramels and toasting nuts.

Maybe you are looking for new ideas for school lunch boxes, or wondering what to bake with all those just-gathered apples or blackberries... even butternut squash and courgettes? This chapter holds the answers.

After a long autumnal walk, a cup of tea and a plate of freshly baked Treacly Ginger Nuts, or another slice of Coffee, Cardamom and Walnut Cake, seems just right. For a gathering, bake my Blackberry, Apple and Cobnut Crumble Cake, while the Poire William Mousse Cake makes a dazzling end to a dinner party. Wondering what to serve with the fireworks or at Hallowe'en? Try Sticky Toffee Apple Fairy Cakes or Crescent Moons... or the ghoulish will adore Witches' Cheesy Fingers.

coffee, cardamom and walnut cake

A twist on an old favourite, the exotic addition of freshly crushed cardamom to this cake is sublime. I've also put in a few ground almonds to make an extra-moist cake.

Serves 6

FOR THE CAKE

175g unsalted butter, really soft, in pieces, plus more for the tins

50g walnuts, roughly chopped

15 cardamom pods

175g caster sugar

1 tbsp instant coffee, dissolved in 1 tbsp of boiling water and cooled

3 eggs, lightly beaten

50g ground almonds

125g self-raising flour, sifted

FOR THE CARAMELISED WALNUTS

50g walnut halves

100g caster sugar

FOR THE BUTTERCREAM

5 cardamom pods

150g unsalted butter, softened, in pieces

250g icing sugar, sifted

1 tsp vanilla extract

2 tsp Camp coffee essence (or 1 tbsp instant coffee, prepared as above for the cake)

1 tbsp double cream

Preheat the oven to 180°C/fan 160°C/350°F/gas mark 4. Butter two 20cm round sandwich tins and line with baking parchment. Keeping them separate, place the nuts both for the cake and the caramelised nuts on baking trays and roast for six minutes. Cool.

Lay the walnut halves for the caramelised walnuts on a baking tray lined with baking parchment. Have a sink or washing-up bowl of cold water to hand. Put the sugar and 100ml of cold water in a saucepan and dissolve the sugar over a gentle heat, stirring with a metal spoon. Increase the heat to a boil, stop stirring and occasionally brush the sides of the pan with a pastry brush dipped in cold water, to prevent crystals forming. Boil until the mixture turns a beautiful caramel gold and has thickened. Plunge the base of the pan into the cold water, then, using a teaspoon, drizzle the caramel over the walnuts on the tray and leave to set.

De-seed all 20 cardamom pods for the cake and buttercream, grind the seeds to a powder in a mortar and pestle and sift it to remove husks. Keep one-quarter aside for the buttercream.

In a food mixer (or in a bowl with a hand-held electric whisk), cream together the butter, sugar and coffee until very light and fluffy (a good five minutes). Gradually add the eggs, then the almonds and cardamom. Gently fold in the flour and chopped nuts; don't over-mix. Divide between the tins and bake for 20–25 minutes, or until a skewer comes out clean. Cool on a wire rack.

To make the buttercream, in a food mixer (or in a bowl with a hand-held electric whisk), beat the butter and icing sugar for a good five minutes. Add the vanilla extract, cardamom, coffee and cream and beat until smooth. Spread over both cakes, then place one on top of the other. Spread it over the sides, too, if you like. Decorate with caramelised walnuts and shards of the caramel, to make a dramatic autumnal decoration.

poire william mousse cake

A stunning autumnal dessert cake, light and heavenly, with a fabulous gingernut biscuit base. Despite appearances, this really isn't difficult to create. Both cake and decoration can be made the day before. The mousse works equally well as a lemon mousse, using lemon juice instead of Poire William.

Serves 10

FOR THE BASE

60g unsalted butter, melted, plus
   more for the tin
300g ginger nut biscuits
   (or dark chocolate digestives,
   if you prefer)

FOR THE MOUSSE

3 gelatine leaves (2g per sheet)
3 egg yolks, at room temperature
80g golden caster sugar
100ml Poire William liqueur
500ml double cream

FOR THE CANDIED PEAR SLICES

a little vegetable oil (optional)
6 tbsp caster sugar
2–3 firm pears

Preheat the oven to 180°C/fan 160°C/350°F/gas mark 4. Flip the base of a 23cm round springform tin so the lip faces down (or you'll struggle to remove the cake). Butter the sides and base. Place the biscuits in a bag and bash with a rolling pin to fine crumbs. Tip into a bowl and mix in the butter. Press into the tin with the back of a spoon and bake for 15 minutes. Leave to cool.

Place the gelatine in a bowl of cold water and soak for five minutes until soft. Meanwhile, place the egg yolks and sugar in a bowl and, using a hand-held electric whisk, or in a food mixer, whisk until the mixture reaches the 'ribbon stage' (see page 18).

In a pan, gently warm the Poire William to blood temperature (check with your finger; do not over-heat). Remove from the heat. Squeeze the gelatine to remove the water and stir into the Poire William until dissolved. Cool slightly, and fold into the mousse. Whip the cream to soft peaks and fold into the mousse. You need to keep it all as light as possible, so be gentle. Pour over the base, cover with cling film and chill for several hours, or overnight.

Preheat the oven to 100°C/fan 80°C/210°F/gas mark ¼. Gather two silicone sheets, or very lightly oil baking parchment on two baking trays. Place the sugar and 2 tbsp of water in a pan over a low heat. Stir until the sugar dissolves, then increase the heat. Boil for a minute or two, then cool slightly. Very thinly slice the pears, dry with kitchen paper, dip into the syrup and lay on the trays. Cook for one hour, then turn and cook for 30 minutes, or until slightly dried out and sticky. Remove to a wire rack. The slices will crisp up. Store in dry conditions in a tin, not in a steamy kitchen.

When ready to serve, run a knife dipped in hot water around the rim of the tin and release the spring. Ease off the base with a palette knife and slide on to a serving plate. Decorate with the pear slices and serve. (Do not return to the fridge.)

chocolate, peanut and salted caramel squares

I wanted to create my own home-made biscuit-based version of that well-known chocolate bar combining chocolate, peanut and caramel. Judging by how popular these are, I think I have succeeded! If peanuts are not for you, simply leave them out for a more classic millionaire's shortbread.

Makes 16

FOR THE SHORTBREAD

250g unsalted butter, slightly soft, plus more for the tin

300g plain flour, sifted

½ tsp salt

100g golden icing sugar, sifted

1 tsp vanilla extract

FOR THE SALTED PEANUT CARAMEL, EITHER

140g light muscovado sugar

400g can condensed milk

140g unsalted butter

80g salted peanuts, chopped

½ tsp salt (optional)

OR

1½ x 450g jars of dulce de leche

½–1 tsp salt (optional)

80g salted peanuts, chopped

FOR THE CHOCOLATE LAYER

150g 55–70% cocoa solids chocolate, finely chopped

200ml double cream

60g smooth peanut butter (softened slightly in a microwave or by standing the piping bag in warm water)

TOOLS

piping bag

Lightly butter a 20cm square, loose-based tin.

Place all the shortbread ingredients in a bowl and knead by hand, or tip everything into a food processor and blitz. Don't over-work, or you will toughen the biscuit. Press the shortbread into the prepared tin, prick all over with a fork and chill for an hour or so in the fridge. When ready to bake, preheat the oven to 180°C/fan 160°C/350°F/gas mark 4 and bake for 35–40 minutes, or until pale gold. Cool, in the tin, on a wire rack.

To make the peanut caramel, combine the sugar, condensed milk and butter in a heavy-based pan. Melt over a medium-low heat, then simmer very gently for five or six minutes, stirring all the time, until it thickens (stir assiduously, as it will scorch easily). Tip in the peanuts, and salt to taste (if needed). Pour over the shortbread, cool and leave to set for an hour or so in the fridge. (Or simply mix the dulce de leche and salt, if using, and stir in the nuts.)

For the chocolate layer, place the chocolate in a bowl. Bring the cream to a boil in a small pan and pour it over the chocolate. Leave for a couple of minutes, then stir until smooth.

Pour the chocolate over the caramel and leave to set. Spoon the smooth peanut butter into a piping bag and snip off the end. Pipe a pattern of your choice (I piped autumn leaves) on each square.

These will keep for a few days in an airtight container.

giant smartie cookies

Chewy, chocolatey and studded with everyone's favourite sweet!

Makes 12

200g unsalted butter, softened,
   in pieces

250g light muscovado sugar

2 tbsp golden syrup

1 egg, plus 1 egg yolk, lightly
   beaten together

1 tsp vanilla extract

320g plain flour, sifted, plus
   more to dust

1 tsp baking powder

100g white chocolate chips

4 x 38g tubes of Smarties

Preheat the oven to 180°C/fan 160°C/350°F/gas mark 4.
Line two large baking trays, or three smaller trays, with
baking parchment.

Beat the butter, sugar and syrup with a hand-held electric whisk
until light and fluffy, then beat in the egg and egg yolk and vanilla
extract. Fold in the flour, baking powder and chocolate chips.

Lightly flour your hands and roughly divide the mixture into
12 pieces. Roll each into a ball and place 4cm apart on the
prepared trays. Squash each down with your fingers and press in
a generous amount of Smarties per cookie. (I used about 10.)

Bake in the preheated oven for 15–17 minutes; they will be a
lovely golden brown, but still not cooked completely in the centre
as they continue to harden out of the oven.

Leave to cool on the baking trays for a few minutes, then place on
a wire rack. These will store in an airtight container for a few days,
if they get the chance…

date, oat and hazelnut fingers

If you can find semi-dried dates they would be even more delicious in this recipe.

Makes 15

100g unsalted butter, in pieces,
   slightly softened, plus more
   for the tin
80g hazelnuts
250g ready-to-eat dates, pitted
   and chopped
2 dessert apples, peeled, cored
   and chopped
finely grated zest and juice of
   1½ large organic oranges
80g light muscovado sugar
180g plain flour, sifted
pinch of salt
100g rolled oats

Preheat the oven to 170°C/fan 150°C/340°F/gas mark 3½. Lightly butter a 30 x 23cm tray bake tin or Swiss roll tray.

Place the hazelnuts on a baking tray and cook in the preheated oven for five minutes or so, watching carefully. Remove them when they are lightly roasted. Let cool slightly, chop finely, then set aside.

Place the dates, apples and orange zest and juice in a pan and set over a low heat. Simmer together, stirring every now and then, until soft. Cool. (If using semi-dried dates, cook the apples and oranges together first, adding the dates at the end for only a minute or so.) Mash together lightly with a fork. Set aside.

Place the sugar, butter, flour, salt and rolled oats in a bowl. Rub together with your fingertips until the mixture resembles crumbs, then add the hazelnuts.

Press half the oat mixture into the prepared tin or tray, then spread the date mixture all over, and finally top with another layer of oat mixture. Bake in the preheated oven for 25–30 minutes, until golden brown.

Cool completely in the tin or tray and cut into 15 fingers to serve.

ginger tray bake

This lovely moist cake is perfect for back-to-school lunch boxes. It is just as delicious without the lemon-ginger glaze; in fact my daughter prefers it that way.

Makes 20 squares

FOR THE CAKE

170g unsalted butter, in pieces, plus more for the tin

230g golden syrup

230g dark muscovado sugar

280g self-raising flour

1 tsp mixed spice

2–3 tsp ground ginger

1 tsp ground cinnamon

pinch of salt

2 eggs, lightly beaten

200ml milk, at room temperature

FOR THE LEMON-GINGER GLAZE

250g icing sugar (golden if you prefer), sifted

2–4 tbsp ginger syrup from the stem ginger jar (optional)

2–3 tbsp lemon juice

2 pieces stem ginger, finely chopped

Preheat the oven to 180°C/fan 160°C/350°F/gas mark 4. Lightly butter a 30 x 23cm tray bake tin and line the base with baking parchment.

Place the butter, syrup and sugar in a pan and heat gently until melted. Remove from the heat and allow to cool a little.

Sift the flour and all the spices and salt into a large bowl. Using a large metal or wooden spoon, stir into the slightly cooled syrup mixture, then add the eggs, and finally pour in the milk, stirring gently as you do so.

Pour into the prepared tin and bake in the preheated oven for 35–40 minutes, or until well risen. A skewer should come out clean, or the cake spring back to the touch. Leave to cool in the tin for a few minutes, then turn out on to a wire rack until cold.

To make the glaze, place the icing sugar in a bowl and gradually add the ginger syrup, if using, and the lemon juice, until you have a smooth spreadable consistency. Pour over the cake, spread with a palette knife and sprinkle over the stem ginger.

Leave to set, then cut into 20 squares. The cake stores well in an airtight container for a few days.

treacly ginger nuts

While visiting my sister-in-law in Connecticut a few years ago, especially to see the exquisite fall colours, she made a batch of these cookies. They're excellent for dunking into warming cups of tea.

Makes 30

170g unsalted butter, in pieces,
  plus more for the trays
  (optional)
260g plain flour
2 tsp ground cinnamon
2 tsp ground ginger
½ tsp mixed spice
2 tsp bicarbonate of soda
180g light muscovado sugar
140g treacle
1 egg, lightly beaten
3–4 tbsp demerara sugar

Line two baking trays with baking parchment, or butter them well. Sift together the flour, cinnamon, ginger, mixed spice and bicarbonate of soda.

With a hand-held electric whisk, beat the butter and sugar until light and fluffy, beat in the treacle and egg, then add the flour mixture. Cover with cling film and chill for 30 minutes to firm up. Preheat the oven to 180°C/fan 160°C/350°F/gas mark 4.

Divide the dough into 30 walnut-sized pieces and place on the prepared trays, spacing them fairly well apart as they will spread. Lightly flatten them with your hand, sprinkle with the demerara sugar and bake in the preheated oven for eight to 10 minutes. They harden as they cool, so don't over-bake them!

Cool on a wire rack, then store in an airtight tin, where they will keep well for a few days.

maple and pecan autumn leaves

Wondering how to use my little tin of metal leaf cutters, I created these nutty biscuits filled with maple buttercream. Sit by the fireside with a plate of these while the wind howls around outside.

Makes about 50 leaves
(25 sandwiches)

FOR THE PECAN BISCUITS

50g pecan nuts

200g plain flour, plus more
    to dust

1 tsp ground cinnamon

60g light muscovado sugar

125g unsalted butter, softened,
    in pieces

FOR THE MAPLE BUTTERCREAM

100g unsalted butter, softened,
    in pieces

150g icing sugar, sifted, plus
    more to dust

1 tsp vanilla extract

1 tbsp golden syrup

1 tbsp maple syrup

TOOLS

set of leaf cutters (mine are
    3–5cm long)

Line two baking trays with baking parchment. Tip the nuts on to a baking tray and cook for five minutes, or until lightly roasted. Let cool slightly, then chop very, very finely. Set aside.

Sift together the flour and cinnamon, add the sugar and rub in the butter with your fingertips until it resembles crumbs. Add the nuts and continue to work; it will come together as a dough.

On a very lightly floured work top, roll out the dough to 3–4mm thick. Cut out the biscuits with the leaf cutters, remembering to make an even number of each shape, as you will be sandwiching them together. At this point, you can freeze the cut-out biscuits.

Lay the biscuits on the prepared baking trays and rest in the fridge for 30 minutes. Preheat the oven to 180°C/fan 160°C/350°F/ gas mark 4. Bake the biscuits for 15–20 minutes, until they are a lovely pale gold. Cool on the trays to firm up for about five minutes, then transfer to a wire rack with a palette knife to cool completely. The unfilled biscuits will keep well for several days in an airtight tin, but once filled need to be served on the day.

Meanwhile, to make the buttercream, place the butter, icing sugar, vanilla and golden syrup in a bowl and, using a hand-held electric whisk, beat for four or five minutes until paler and creamy. Drizzle in the maple syrup and beat thoroughly.

When ready to serve, sandwich the leaves together with the buttercream and dust with a sprinkling of icing sugar.

blackberry, apple and cobnut crumble cake

This cake combines the essential flavours of autumn's harvest and is deeply comforting. Hazelnuts can be used if cobnuts are not available. Serve warm from the oven, with a bowl of crème fraîche. If you don't want to make the crumble topping, simply sprinkle 2 tbsp of demerara sugar over the cake before baking.

Serves 8

FOR THE CAKE

200g unsalted butter, melted and cooled, plus more for the tin

280g self-raising flour

2 tsp baking powder

1 tsp salt

1 tsp ground ginger

2 tsp ground cinnamon

2 dessert apples

juice and finely grated zest of ½ unwaxed lemon

250g golden caster sugar

3 eggs, lightly beaten

1 tsp vanilla extract

100ml whole milk

250g blackberries

FOR THE CRUMBLE

100g unsalted butter, chilled and cut into pieces

150g plain flour, sifted

80g light muscovado sugar

½ tsp ground cinnamon

handful (about 50g) of roughly chopped cobnuts or hazelnuts

Preheat the oven to 180°C/fan 160°C/350°F/gas mark 4. Butter a 23cm round springform tin and line the base with baking parchment.

Make the crumble topping first: in a large bowl, rub the butter, flour, sugar and cinnamon together into fine crumbs with your fingertips (if this is over-mixed in a food mixer, it quickly turns to biscuit dough).

For the cake, sift the flour, baking powder, salt, ginger and cinnamon into a large bowl. Peel, core and dice the apples finely and separately toss them in the lemon juice and zest. Set aside.

In another large bowl, using a hand-held electric whisk, or in a food mixer, beat the sugar, cooled melted butter, eggs and vanilla until thick and creamy; this will take a few minutes on high speed. With a large spoon, fold in the flour mixture, alternating with the milk. Don't over-mix.

Spoon the batter into the prepared tin, then scatter the apples and blackberries over the surface and gently push them in. Sprinkle over the crumble, top with the nuts and bake in the preheated oven for 50–60 minutes, or until a skewer comes out clean.

Cool the cake in the tin for about 10 minutes, then remove from the tin and serve. If making ahead, cool completely on a wire rack, then slightly warm through to serve.

white chocolate and blackberry fingers

Perfect for an autumnal afternoon tea or supper. If you don't have a blackberry bush to hand, then of course you can buy cultivated ones. (Not the same thing, but a very good second best.) Raspberries and blueberries could always be used instead, if you prefer. When making ganache, you must use a good-quality white chocolate that will thicken up sufficiently in the ganache mixture. I like to use Swiss white chocolate as I find it works reliably.

Makes 10

FOR THE SHORTBREAD

150g slightly salted butter, slightly softened, in pieces, plus more for the tin

60g golden icing sugar

150g plain flour

75g cornflour

FOR THE GANACHE

200g good-quality white chocolate, very finely chopped

200ml double cream

300g blackberries

FOR THE TOPPING (OPTIONAL)

a few toasted flaked almonds

a little crème de cassis

TOOLS (OPTIONAL)

piping bag fitted with star nozzle

Preheat the oven to 180°C/fan 160°C/350°F/gas mark 4. Lightly butter a 20cm square tin.

First of all, make the ganache. Place the chocolate in a bowl. Bring the cream just to a boil in a small pan, then pour it over the chocolate. Leave for a minute, then stir gently until smooth. Let it cool, then chill for a good hour or two. When it has chilled, whisk the ganache with a hand-held electric whisk until it thickens.

To make this buttery shortbread, I think it is best to use your hands. Place the butter in a large bowl and add the sugar. Sift in the flour and cornflour and knead together until it binds. Press gently into the prepared tin, prick all over with a fork and bake in the preheated oven for 35–40 minutes, or until golden brown. Cool for a few minutes, then score into 10 fingers.

Both the shortbreads and the ganache can be made a day or so in advance (although it has to be said, there is nothing like freshly baked, just-cooled shortbread!).

To serve, divide the ganache between the just-cool shortbreads (pipe it on, if you like) and scatter with blackberries. For the optional topping, add the flaked almonds and a light drizzle of crème de cassis just before serving.

spiced butternut mini loaf cakes

For this cake, you'll need 10 mini loaf cardboard cases (each 5.5 x 4cm), from big supermarkets or good kitchen supply shops. If you can't find them, this recipe will also make 16 muffins. Bake the muffins, at the same oven temperature, for 18–20 minutes.

*Makes 10 mini loaves,
or 16 muffins*

300g plain flour

½ tsp salt

2 tsp baking powder

½ tsp bicarbonate of soda

1 tsp ground ginger

1 tsp ground cinnamon

1 tsp ground nutmeg

240g butternut squash,
  prepared weight

1 really ripe banana

150g unsalted butter, very soft

150g light muscovado sugar

75ml vegetable oil

2 eggs, lightly beaten

FOR THE TOPPING

50g pecan nuts

4 tbsp maple syrup

Preheat the oven to 190°C/fan 170°C/375°F/gas mark 5. Tip the nuts for the topping on to a baking tray and place in the oven for five minutes, or until lightly roasted. Cool slightly, then finely chop and set aside.

Sift together the flour, salt, baking powder, bicarbonate of soda, ginger, cinnamon and nutmeg in a large bowl.

Grate the squash, place in a tea towel and wring to remove excess water. Mash the banana in a small bowl, then mix in the squash.

Cream the butter and sugar together until really light and creamy, using a food mixer or a hand-held electric whisk. Stir in the squash, banana and oil. Fold in the flour mixture a couple of spoonfuls at a time, alternating with the eggs.

Divide between the loaf cases and bake for 20–25 minutes or until well-risen and golden. Cool in the cases on a wire rack.

When cool, mix the pecan nuts with the maple syrup and spoon over the cakes.

chocolate courgette cake

The courgettes give this chocolate cake a lovely, moist texture… people will never guess what the secret ingredient is, unless you choose to tell them. During autumn, a new recipe for something to do with a glut of courgettes is a godsend.

Serves 16

FOR THE CAKE

120g unsalted butter, really soft, in pieces, plus more for the tin

300g plain flour

4 tbsp cocoa, plus more to dust

½ tsp baking powder

1 tsp bicarbonate of soda

1 tsp ground cinnamon

¼ tsp salt

140ml sunflower oil

400g caster sugar

2 eggs, lightly beaten

1 tsp vanilla extract

140ml buttermilk, at room temperature

180g peeled and grated courgettes, excess water squeezed out (prepared weight)

150g 70% cocoa solids chocolate, finely chopped

Preheat the oven to 170°C/fan 150°C/340°F/gas mark 3½. Butter a 23cm square tin and line the base with baking parchment.

Sift together the flour, cocoa, baking powder, bicarbonate of soda, cinnamon and salt.

In the bowl of a food mixer (or in a bowl with a hand-held electric whisk), cream together the butter, oil and sugar until very light and fluffy (this will take a good five minutes). Gradually add the eggs, vanilla extract and buttermilk. Gently fold in the flour mixture, followed by the courgettes and chocolate, and blend well together, being careful not to over-mix.

Pour the batter into the prepared tin and bake in the preheated oven for 55–60 minutes. Let cool in the tin for a few minutes before turning out on to a wire rack to cool completely.

Sift over a little cocoa, cut into 16 squares and serve

sugar plum crumble fairy cakes

Use sweet, flavourful, ripe plums. I like to mix in some damsons too if I have them (I am lucky enough to have a neighbour's damson branch leaning into our garden!) In fact any mixture of plums, blackberries and even slices of apple work well. These are best served warm with crème fraîche.

Makes 20

FOR THE CRUMBLE TOPPING

80g plain flour

50g unsalted butter, slightly chilled, in pieces

30g demerara sugar

FOR THE CAKES

250g plain flour

2 tsp baking powder

2 tsp ground cinnamon

½ tsp salt

130g unsalted butter, really soft

200g golden caster sugar

3 eggs, lightly beaten

1 tsp vanilla extract

250ml buttermilk, at room temperature

6–7 plums, pitted and chopped

Preheat the oven to 180°C/fan 160°C/350°F/gas mark 4. Place 20 fairy cake cases into two fairy cake tins.

To make the crumble, in a large bowl, rub together the flour and butter with your fingertips to form crumbs, then stir in the sugar. Set aside. For the cakes, sift the flour, baking powder, cinnamon and salt into another bowl and set aside separately.

Cream together the butter and sugar for a few minutes until really light and fluffy. Gradually add the eggs, with 1 tbsp of the flour mixture so it doesn't curdle. Add the vanilla, then alternately fold in the flour mixture and buttermilk. Spoon the batter into the cases and top each with the plums and a spoonful of the crumble.

Bake in the preheated oven for 15–20 minutes, until they are golden brown and spring back to the touch.

fig, blackcurrant and fennel tarts

Deep purply, plump and lusciously sweet black Bursa figs from Turkey appear during late summer and autumn. Gone are the days when I always made my puff pastry; I must admit I often buy it these days. But rough puff is much less scary and I urge you to make it; the textured layers are out of this world. The pastry recipe is more than doubled so, as it freezes brilliantly, cut off 500g to make the tarts and keep the rest in the freezer for another time.

Makes 8

EITHER

FOR THE ROUGH PUFF PASTRY

500g plain flour, sifted, plus
   more to dust

500g slightly salted butter, quite
   cold, cut into pieces

OR

500g ready-made all-butter
   puff pastry

FOR THE TOPPING

1 tbsp fennel seeds, plus a few
   more to sprinkle

2 tbsp crème de cassis, or good
   fresh blackcurrant cordial

6–8 ripe figs

50g unsalted butter, melted

100–120g golden caster sugar

To make the pastry, place the flour in a large bowl and coarsely rub in the butter (there should still be pieces of butter). Form a well in the centre and add 200–250ml of iced water, just enough for a firm dough. Wrap in cling film and chill for 15 minutes.

On a lightly floured work top (ideally marble), roll out the dough to 50 x 20cm. You should be able to see the pieces of butter still. Fold into three, as you would a letter, turn it 90 degrees and roll out again to a large rectangle as before. Fold into three once more, wrap in cling film and chill for 20 minutes. Repeat this whole process of rolling and folding twice more, resting between each. I know it seems long-winded, but you may become hooked; it is a rewarding process (even more so to eat).

Meanwhile, grind the 1 tbsp of fennel seeds to a powder in a mortar and pestle, sift, then mix with the cassis. Cut each fig into 10. Turn them in the cassis and leave for 30 minutes.

Line two baking trays with baking parchment. On a floured board, roll out 500g of the pastry to about 4mm thick. Cut out eight 10cm circles. Place on the trays, spaced apart. Chill for 30 minutes. Preheat the oven to 220°C/fan 200°C/425°F/gas mark 7.

To bake the tarts, prick the pastry all over with a fork, leaving a border, and arrange the figs in a circle, again leaving a border. Brush the figs generously with melted butter and sprinkle each tart with 1 tbsp of sugar (this will caramelise in the oven). Scatter over a few fennel seeds. Bake for 15–18 minutes until golden. Immediately remove to a wire rack, or the caramel will stick to the trays, and serve within an hour or two.

rosehip syrup

Our hedgerows are filled with bushes laden with elderberries and sloes. Each year I gather them to make delicious drinks which last all winter. The glowing red rosehips I ignored, until I was given this recipe by Julia Thompson, a medicinal herbalist who lives in the neighbouring village. Packed full of vitamin C, drizzle it over fruits as a syrup, or serve as a cordial diluted with sparkling water.

Makes 900ml–1.2 litres

1kg fresh-gathered bright red rosehips, thoroughly washed
500g caster sugar

Rinse the rosehips and lightly crush them (this is easiest in a food processor). Boil a kettle. Place the hips in a large pan and pour over 1.7 litres of boiling water. Return to a boil over a high heat, then leave to stand for about 15 minutes.

Strain the liquid through a sieve lined with a double layer of fine muslin over another pan. When it has stopped dripping, return the rosehips to the original pan with another 900ml of boiling water. As you did before, return to a boil and leave to stand for 15 minutes. Strain as before and add to the first extract. Strain once again, ensuring all the very tiny fine hairs are removed.

Pour into a clean pan and boil to reduce to 900ml–1.2 litres. Add the sugar and stir over a gentle heat, allowing it all to dissolve, then increase the heat and bring to a boil. Pour into sterilised small bottles (see page 27) and seal. Once open, use it quickly.

sloe gin

Wait until the sloe bushes have been frosted, or cheat and place the berries overnight in the freezer for the same result: the berries will soften. Classically you are supposed to prick each berry with a needle, but I can never be bothered!

Makes about 750ml

1.5kg sloes, thoroughly washed and dried
700ml bottle of gin
400g granulated sugar

Pack the sloes into a two-litre Kilner jar. Pour over the gin and add the sugar. Seal firmly, shake and leave in a cool, dark place.

Shake every week for at least three months. Strain through a sieve lined with muslin and pour into sterilised bottles (see page 27). The gin improves with keeping, so try doubling the recipe if you get a good haul of sloes.

elderberry cordial

A deep purple spiced cordial from the hedgerow that is said to hold huge health benefits. Some claim it guards against flu. Whether it does or not, it has been made for centuries and is utterly delicious.

Makes about 1.7 litres

2kg elderberries, thoroughly washed

about 900g–1.3kg caster or granulated sugar

juice of about 2–3 unwaxed lemons and their pared zest (no pith)

5–6 tbsp grated root ginger

2–3 cinnamon sticks

about 36 cloves

Strip the elderberries from the heads (the easiest way is with a fork). Tip into a saucepan and cover with water. Simmer over a gentle heat for 20–25 minutes, or until tender.

Strain through a sieve lined with muslin, then measure the juice. Pour it into the pan. For each 600ml of juice, add 450g of sugar, the juice and zest of 1 lemon, 2 tbsp grated ginger, 1 cinnamon stick and 12 cloves. Bring to a boil, stirring to dissolve the sugar, then increase the heat and boil hard for 10 minutes.

Strain and pour into sterilised bottles (see page 27). The cordial will keep well for at least a few months. Serve diluted with hot or cold or sparkling water.

carrot and pineapple cake

Carrot cake is one of our best-loved classics, and here the old-fashioned but brilliantly effective addition of crushed pineapple makes it even more moist.

Serves 10

FOR THE CAKE

unsalted butter, for the tin

140g walnut halves

435g can of pineapple in unsweetened juice, drained

300g self-raising flour

2 tsp baking powder

2 tsp ground cinnamon

pinch of salt

½ tsp mixed spice

4 eggs, lightly beaten

100g golden caster sugar

150g light muscovado sugar

220ml sunflower oil

230g carrots, peeled and finely grated

finely grated zest of 1 lime (organic if possible)

50g desiccated coconut (optional)

edible flowers, to decorate (optional)

FOR THE FROSTING

200g full-fat cream cheese, at room temperature

100g unsalted butter, softened, in pieces

60g icing sugar, sifted

finely grated zest and juice of 1 lime (organic if possible)

Preheat the oven to 180°C/fan 160°C/350°F/gas mark 4. Butter a 23cm round, deep cake tin and line the base and sides with baking parchment.

Place the walnuts on a baking tray and roast in the oven for six minutes or so. Set aside about 60g and chop them very finely – or pulse-blend in a mini food processor – for the decoration. Roughly chop the rest. Process the drained pineapple to a purée.

Sift together the flour, baking powder, cinnamon, salt and mixed spice and set aside.

In the bowl of a food mixer (or in a bowl with a hand-held electric whisk), beat together the eggs and sugars for two or three minutes, then slowly pour in the oil, still beating.

Squeeze excess moisture from the pineapple in your hands, then fold it in with the carrots, roughly chopped nuts, lime zest, coconut, if using, and lastly the flour mixture, making sure it is well incorporated.

Pour into the prepared tin and bake for 55 minutes, or until a skewer comes out clean. (If the top is browning quickly before the cake is baked, protect the surface with a circle of foil with a hole cut out of the centre. Place it over the cake and fold over the sides of the tin, to protect the edge of the cake.) Cool for a few minutes, then remove from the tin and cool on a wire rack.

To make the frosting, in a bowl, lightly beat the cream cheese and set aside. Separately beat the butter and icing sugar together until light and fluffy. Slowly add the cream cheese, lime zest and juice. Using a palette knife, spread the frosting all over the top and sides of the cake. Sprinkle the finely chopped walnuts in a band around the side and finish with a few edible flowers, if you like (I used marigolds from my garden).

white chocolate and nectarine tart

Best eaten on the day it is baked, the only trick to this recipe is to find the ripest sweet nectarines. The fruits are still around well into the autumn, but this tart would be equally good with sliced figs.

Serves 6

FOR THE PASTRY

80g unsalted butter, chilled, in
  pieces, plus more for the tin
125g plain flour, plus more
  to dust
pinch of salt
1 tsp baking powder
1 tbsp golden caster sugar
50ml double cream
1 egg yolk

FOR THE FILLING

50g blanched hazelnuts
90g unsalted butter
125g golden icing sugar, sifted
150g good-quality white
  chocolate, finely chopped
2 eggs, lightly beaten
60g self-raising flour, sifted
3–4 ripe nectarines, peeled,
  pitted and chopped (about
  220g prepared weight)

Lightly butter a 23cm round loose-bottomed metal flan tin. Sift the flour, salt and baking powder into a bowl and add the sugar and butter, rubbing together with your fingertips (or mixing in a food mixer) until the mixture forms crumbs. Add the cream and egg yolk and mix just until the dough comes together; do not over-mix. Wrap in cling film and rest in the fridge for 30 minutes.

Lightly flour a work top and roll out the pastry to a large circle about 3mm thick. Lift the pastry around the rolling pin and lay it over the tin. Press it in, cutting off the excess. Prick the base with a fork and rest in the fridge for another 30 minutes. Preheat the oven to 190°C/fan 170°C/375°F/gas mark 5. Tip the nuts for the filling on to a baking tray and place in the oven for five minutes, or until lightly roasted. Cool, then grind in a mini food processor.

Line the pastry case with a large circle of baking parchment and fill with ceramic baking beans or raw rice. Cook for 15 minutes, then remove the beans and paper and return to the oven for another five minutes or so, until pale gold. (This is called 'blind baking', and part-cooks the pastry so the base won't be soggy.)

To make the filling, melt the butter over a very low heat, then stir in the sugar and 100g of the chocolate. Cool a little, then beat in the eggs gradually, followed by the ground hazelnuts and flour. Tip into the pastry case. Scatter over the nectarines, drained of any liquid, then press gently into the filling, so they are half-covered.

Return to the oven and bake for 30–40 minutes, until golden and set. Cool on a wire rack, then carefully remove from the tin.

When cold, melt the remaining white chocolate in a heatproof bowl over gently simmering water, ensuring the bowl does not touch the water. Drizzle it over the tart and serve slightly warm.

sticky toffee apple fairy cakes

Hand out a tray of these at your next bonfire party, deliciously moist and sticky with both apples and dates and a toffee topping. It's an easy mixture, all made in one pan, and will delight everyone. Try to find black or dark brown fairy cake cases, and gather 20 very clean twigs (or lolly sticks).

Makes 20

FOR THE CHOCOLATE LEAVES

50g 60% cocoa solids chocolate, chopped

FOR THE CAKES

1 dessert apple

finely grated zest of ½ unwaxed lemon, plus a squeeze of its juice

90g dates, pitted and roughly chopped

80g unsalted butter, in pieces

½ tsp bicarbonate of soda

½ tsp vanilla extract

¼ tsp salt

100g light muscovado sugar

½ tsp ground ginger

110g self-raising flour, sifted

1 egg, lightly beaten

FOR THE TOFFEE TOPPING

40g unsalted butter, in pieces

80g light muscovado sugar

60ml double cream

½ tsp vanilla extract

TOOLS

piping bag

To make the chocolate leaves, first place a sheet of baking parchment on to a tray. Melt the chocolate in a small heatproof bowl over very gently simmering water, making sure the bowl does not touch the water. Spoon the chocolate into the piping bag and snip off the tip. Pipe leaf shapes about 3cm long (see photo, right) and leave to dry (a short spell in the fridge will help).

Preheat the oven to 180°C/fan 160°C/350°F/gas mark 4. Place 20 paper fairy cake cases into a couple of fairy cake tins.

Peel, core and grate the apple, squeeze out any juice in your fist, and toss with the lemon zest and a little juice to stop the apple browning. Set aside.

Place the dates in a large heavy-based pan and pour over 90ml of boiling water. Set over a very low heat and simmer, stirring to ensure the dates don't stick to the pan. Once they have softened and broken up a bit (about five minutes), remove from the heat. Tip in the butter and stir until melted, followed by the apple, bicarbonate of soda, vanilla, salt, sugar, ginger and flour, and finally the egg. Mix and divide between the paper cases.

Bake in the preheated oven for 15–20 minutes, until the centres spring back to the touch. Remove and cool completely on a wire rack. These cakes will freeze well (without the topping).

For the topping, simmer the ingredients together over a low heat, stirring all the time to stop it scorching, until thickened and caramel brown. Cool slightly, then pour over the cakes.

Stick a twig or lolly stick into each cake. Very carefully peel a chocolate leaf or two from the baking parchment and decorate some of the cakes with the leaves. (They are very fragile so this needs to be done at the last minute.) Serve.

spooky chocolate cupcakes

Children will love to create these, and they are guaranteed to be a hit at any spooky Hallowe'en gathering. I've made three designs: cobwebs, spiders and pumpkins. This recipe also makes a good 20cm square chocolate cake for children (bake it for 25–30 minutes).

Makes 12

FOR THE CAKES

125g self-raising flour

30g cocoa

1 tsp baking powder

125g unsalted butter, really soft

150g caster sugar

1 egg, lightly beaten

1 tsp vanilla extract

250ml semi-skimmed or whole
milk, at room temperature

FOR THE ICING

100g orange-flavoured and
coloured chocolate buttons,
or white chocolate,
finely chopped

orange food colour paste

100g chocolate drops
(or 50% cocoa solids
chocolate, finely chopped)

TO DECORATE PUMPKINS

2 liquorice wheels

green mini chocolate beans

TO DECORATE SPIDERS

chocolate sprinkles

chocolate popping candy
(optional)

2 liquorice wheels

red mini chocolate beans

TOOLS

2 piping bags

Preheat the oven to 180°C/fan 160°C/350°F/gas mark 4. Place 12 cupcake cases into a cupcake tray.

To make the cakes, sift together the flour, cocoa and baking powder. In a food mixer, or in a large bowl using a hand-held electric whisk, cream together the butter and sugar until light and fluffy for about five minutes. Beat in the egg and vanilla extract, then add the flour mixture gradually, alternating with the milk, taking care not to over-mix. Divide between the cases. Bake in the oven for 20–25 minutes, or until the cakes spring back to the touch. Leave in the tin for a few minutes, then cool on a wire rack.

Place the orange buttons, or white chocolate, into a heatproof bowl and stand it over simmering water, ensuring the bowl does not touch the water. Colour it orange with a tiny amount of food colour. Spread on six cakes (or all 12 if making 12 pumpkins).

Melt the other chocolate in the same way and use it to cover the remaining six cakes (unless making 12 pumpkins). Take 2 tbsp of both colours of the remaining chocolate and place into piping bags, snipping the ends off. Decorate just a few cakes at a time, as the spirals, liquorice and sprinkles need to stick to wet icing.

For cobwebs, draw a spiral with dark chocolate on the just-iced orange cakes; I find it easiest to pipe from the centre. Using a cocktail stick, drag lines from the middle to form a cobweb. Pipe orange spirals on the dark chocolate cakes in the same way.

For pumpkins, cut eyes and mouths from strips of liquorice wheels and create a green stalk using green mini chocolate beans.

To make spiders, scatter over chocolate sprinkles and a few chocolate popping candy pieces, cutting a few strips of liquorice wheels for legs and adding red mini chocolate beans for eyes.

witches' cheesy fingers

Hugely fun, these are a welcome addition to any Hallowe'en party! Children, especially, love them.

Makes 24

24 well-shaped flaked almonds

red food colour paste

plain flour, to dust

100g finely grated cheddar
   cheese

2 good pinches of cayenne
   pepper or paprika

250g all-butter ready-rolled
   puff pastry, lightly chilled

poppy seeds

TOOLS

paintbrush

Line two baking trays with baking parchment. Paint the flaked almonds with the red food colour paste, using the paintbrush. You'll need well-shaped almonds, as these will form the witches' fingernails. Set aside.

Dust a work top with flour and evenly sprinkle with one-quarter of the finely grated cheese and a pinch of cayenne or paprika. Place half the pastry on top and sprinkle over one-quarter more of the cheese. Dust the rolling pin with a little more flour and roll the pastry to a 30 x 12cm rectangle about 3mm thick. Repeat with the second half of the pastry

Cut into finger-sized strips, each about 12cm long. Roll each 'finger' and, using a very sharp knife, score the pastry to form 'knuckles'. Dip one end of each in poppy seeds to form the 'dried blood' of severed fingers. Insert a red almond fingernail into the other end. Place on the baking trays and rest in the fridge for 30 minutes.

Preheat the oven to 200°C/fan 180°C/400°F/gas mark 6. Bake the fingers for 10–12 minutes. Allow to cool on the baking trays for a couple of minutes, then transfer to a wire rack.

These are best eaten on the day of baking, but they will store for a day or two in an airtight tin.

parkin

Traditionally made in the North of England and served on Bonfire Night, these parkin squares look magnificent piled up on a platter and decorated with mini cake sparklers. Or serve them warmed through with vanilla or toffee ice cream for pudding. Store well wrapped in baking parchment, and seal in an airtight tin, for up to a week for an even stickier and more delicious parkin.

Makes 9 squares

125g unsalted butter, plus more
  for the tin

125g dark muscovado sugar

225g treacle

½ tsp bicarbonate of soda

150g plain flour

2 tsp ground ginger

½ tsp ground nutmeg

pinch of ground cloves

1 tsp baking powder

200g medium oatmeal

50–60ml milk, plus more
  if needed

Preheat the oven to 170°C/fan 150°C/340°F/gas mark 3½. Butter a 20cm square tin and line the base and sides with baking parchment.

In a saucepan, melt the butter, sugar and treacle and heat gently until melted. Add the bicarbonate of soda and allow to cool slightly for around 10 minutes.

In a large mixing bowl, sift the flour, ginger, nutmeg, cloves and baking powder, then add the oatmeal.

Stir the syrup mixture gently into the dry ingredients, adding enough milk to make a very moist batter. (The oatmeal will absorb a lot of moisture while baking, so the batter needs to be very wet.) Pour into the prepared tin and bake in the preheated oven for 50–60 minutes, or until a skewer comes out clean.

Cool in the tin for 20 minutes, then turn out on to a wire rack. Let cool completely and cut into nine squares to serve.

crescent moons

Great for any moonlit bonfire party. Make full moons if you prefer (little round biscuits), which, later in the year, can gain new life rebranded as snowballs.

Makes 40

100g unblanched almonds

230g unsalted butter, softened,
   in pieces

80g golden caster sugar

200g plain flour, sifted

60g cornflour, sifted

pinch of salt

1 tsp anise seeds, ground
   (optional)

½ tsp almond extract

about 50g icing sugar, plus more
   to dust, plus more to store

Preheat the oven to 180°C/fan 160°C/350°F/gas mark 4. Line three baking trays with baking parchment. Place the almonds on a baking sheet and cook for five minutes, until lightly roasted. Cool, then grind finely in a mini food processor.

In the bowl of a food mixer (or in a bowl with a hand-held electric whisk), cream the butter and sugar until light and fluffy; this could take a good five minutes. Gently fold in the rest of the ingredients (except the icing sugar). Wrap in cling film and rest the dough in the fridge for 15 minutes.

Dust a work top with icing sugar. Take pieces of the dough and roll into small sausage shapes around 5cm long. Curve around your finger to form crescent moons and pinch the ends to taper. The biscuits should be 12–15mm thick once formed so, as you make them, you'll learn how much dough will be needed for each. At this point you can freeze the shaped biscuits.

Lay the biscuits well-spaced apart on the baking trays and bake in the preheated oven for 18–20 minutes. Leave on the trays and, while still warm, sift over half the 50g of icing sugar. Leave to cool completely, then sift over the remaining 25g of icing sugar. (This method coats them well.)

Store in an airtight container filled with icing sugar. They should keep well for a week or two.

autumn celebration cake:
marzipan rosehips, leaves and acorns

Make any autumnal celebration special with this centrepiece crunchy hazelnut meringue with a marshmallowy centre and a creamy chocolate filling. I have decorated it with little marzipan oak leaves, acorns and rosehips. If that's not for you, simply dust the meringue with a little cocoa.

Serves 10

FOR THE MERINGUE

80g blanched hazelnuts

5 egg whites, at room temperature

pinch of salt

280g golden caster sugar

FOR THE CHOCOLATE FILLING

150g 70% cocoa solids chocolate, finely chopped

300ml whipping cream

Preheat the oven to 180°C/fan 160°C/350°F/gas mark 4. Line two baking trays with baking parchment and draw two 20cm circles. Turn the papers upside down on the trays, so the pencil marks face downwards. Tip the hazelnuts on to a baking tray and cook for five minutes, or until lightly roasted. Remove, cool slightly, then chop them finely and set aside.

In a large clean bowl using a hand-held electric whisk, or in a food mixer, whisk the egg whites with the salt to soft peaks. Continue to whisk, adding the sugar a spoonful at a time. The meringue will become marshmallowy and glossy.

Fold in the hazelnuts gently and divide the mixture between the two trays, to fill the circles. Bake for five minutes, then reduce the oven temperature to 140°C/fan 120°C/275°F/gas mark 1 and continue to cook for one hour. Remove and leave to cool.

The meringues can be made ahead and stored in an airtight container for a few days, but they should be assembled only an hour or two before serving.

To make the chocolate filling, place the chocolate in a small heatproof bowl over gently simmering water. Ensure the bowl is not touching the water. Remove from the heat once melted. Whip the cream only until it just begins to thicken (use a hand-held electric whisk and a large mixing bowl, or a food mixer).

Now, lightly stir the still-hot chocolate and, whisking all the time, pour it in a continual stream on to the cream. Once evenly combined, spread it on to the least beautiful meringue, placing the most attractive one on top.

250g natural (undyed) marzipan
(to make your own,
see page 50)

icing sugar, to dust

edible glue

chocolate sprinkles

edible white lustre

FOOD COLOUR PASTES
(ALL SUGARFLAIR)

FOR PALE GREEN

Ice Blue

Egg Yellow

FOR PALE ORANGE

Egg Yellow

Tangerine/Apricot

FOR SOFT BROWN

Egg Yellow

Dark Brown

FOR RED

Tangerine/Apricot

Poppy Red

Dark Brown (a pin prick)

FOR DARK BROWN

Dark Brown

TOOLS

small rolling pin

metal oak leaf cutters

silicone veining mat

ball tool

2 small paintbrushes

The marzipan decorations can be made a few weeks ahead and stored in a box (not in an airtight container or the fridge). To make them, divide the marzipan into five pieces, making the last piece very small. Colour each piece a different colour, using tiny amounts of food colour paste and a cocktail stick (see page 62). I made a pale green, pale orange, soft brown, red, and a very small piece of dark brown (for rosehip calyxes and acorn stalks), in the colours mentioned in the list (see left), but this is just a guide.

To make the leaves, use the pale green, pale orange and soft brown coloured marzipans. Take a piece of one of those colours and, on a work top lightly dusted with icing sugar, roll it out with a small rolling pin to about 2mm thick. Cut out a few oak leaves with the cutters. To vein a leaf, take a marzipan oak leaf and lay it into the veining mat. Press the other side down on to it, then lift it carefully. You have made an edible oak leaf, with very realistic veining, front and back. Using the ball tool, soften the edges. Curl the leaves with your fingers, so they look more realistic, and leave to dry. Repeat to make leaves in all three colours.

To make the acorns, take a piece of pale green marzipan about the same size as an acorn and roll it into an oval acorn shape. Using the ball tool, hollow out a piece of soft brown marzipan and form the acorn cup. Leave the cup to dry for a few hours, then paint it with edible glue and roll it in a plate of chocolate sprinkles. Using another paintbrush, brush the acorn with the lustre for a soft shine, then place it into the acorn cup, securing with edible glue. To make a fine stem for the acorn, roll a very small strand of dark brown marzipan in your fingers, make a small hole in the end of the cup with a cocktail stick and, using the edible glue, attach.

To make the rosehips, roll a piece of the red marzipan into an oval slightly smaller than an acorn. Make a very tiny ball of dark brown marzipan and, using the end of a small paintbrush and a dot of edible glue, attach it to the wider end.

Arrange all the decorations on top of the meringue, and serve.

winter

winter cakes
candied clementines
and gilded gingerbread

For many of us, winter means short, dull grey days, long dark nights and barren trees… It can all seem a bit bleak. But the winter months do have their own particular beauty: now is the time of bright frosty mornings and clear blue skies, snow fall, the comfort of log fires and candlelight and the mellow winter light.

It is also the time when we come together for our winter festivities at Christmas and New Year. Baking, for me, is a central part of this: I love all the planning, my endless lists and the long hours spent in the kitchen.

I've included many recipes to help you get ahead. Every year I make piles of Gingerbread Men and Crumble Mince Pies (or Squares) which I stash in the freezer, ready to bake freshly as I need them.

You will find ideas for every possible occasion. Here are seasonal puddings, rich moist fruit cakes and delightful edible gifts. My Upside Down Clementine and Star Anise Cake, Little Cranberry Ices or much-loved Chocolate Roulade would be perfect at the end of any meal. For original, delicious edible gift ideas, nothing beats a beautifully packaged batch of seasonal Shortbreads or Ginger Florentines. Whether you choose to spend hours in the kitchen, or are time-poor, a cake decorating expert or a novice, here are recipes for everyone to get involved in the kitchen.

dundee cake

This most famous of Scottish cakes originated in the 19th century and was originally made as a mass-produced cake in Scotland by Keiller's, the marmalade company. It has become one of Britain's most-loved fruit cakes, and is lighter than most. This cake can be made a few days ahead; in fact the flavour will improve with keeping.

Serves 8–10

225g unsalted butter, softened, in pieces, plus more for the tin

250g sultanas

100g raisins

100g currants

100g undyed glacé cherries, rinsed, dried and halved

140g self-raising flour

½ tsp salt

1 tsp mixed spice

100g ground almonds

225g dark muscovado sugar

4 eggs, lightly beaten

finely grated zest of 1 unwaxed lemon

1–2 tbsp whisky, or milk

about 60 whole blanched almonds

FOR THE GLAZE

1 tbsp milk

2 tsp caster sugar

Lightly butter a 20cm round, 7.5cm deep cake tin and line with baking parchment. Wrap the outside of the tin with brown paper (or newspaper) and tie with string. This will protect the outside of the cake from drying out, as it will be in the oven for a long time. Preheat the oven to 160°C/fan 140°C/325°F/gas mark 3.

Place the sultanas, raisins, currants and glacé cherries into a bowl and toss with 1–2 tbsp of the flour. Sift the remaining flour, salt and mixed spice into another bowl and add the ground almonds.

Using a food mixer (or a hand-held electric whisk) cream together the butter and sugar for five minutes, until really light and fluffy. Add the eggs gradually, with a spoonful or two of the flour mixture (to prevent it from curdling). Add the lemon zest, all the dried fruits and remaining flour. Using a large spoon, very gently fold everything together, adding the whisky at the end.

Pour the batter into the prepared tin and smooth with a palette knife. Decorate with a few concentric circles of blanched almonds (don't press them down, just place them on lightly) and place in the hot oven. The cake will take 2–2½ hours to bake. If it browns too much before it is cooked, cut a circle of foil, make a hole in the centre and open it out, so the edges are protected. The cake is ready when a skewer comes out almost clean with just a crumb or two on it. Meanwhile, mix together the milk and sugar for the glaze, then brush it evenly over the top. Bake for a final two minutes to set the glaze. Leave to cool completely in the tin.

Store in the cake tin – or wrap in baking parchment and foil – and keep for a few days before eating.

little cranberry ices with ginger lace biscuits

A very refreshing end to a special meal, combining the classic flavours of cinnamon, port and ginger. Both the ices and the biscuits can be made a few days in advance, ready to assemble just before serving. The great thing is that no ice cream machine is needed. If the idea of fiddling with individual portions is not for you, set the ice in one large dish and serve the biscuits separately.

Makes 10

FOR THE ICE

200g fresh cranberries

100ml port

1 cinnamon stick

50ml crème de cassis

6 eggs, separated, at room temperature

250g golden caster sugar

800ml whipping cream, chilled

FOR THE BISCUITS

20g unsalted butter

60ml double cream

30g golden caster sugar

40g unsalted pistachio nuts, roughly chopped

30g stem ginger, finely chopped

40g dried cranberries, roughly chopped

1 tsp plain flour

TO DECORATE

30 fresh cranberries

10 tiny sprigs of rosemary

TOOLS

7.5cm x 3cm deep round metal cutter

For the cranberry ice, place the berries, port and cinnamon in a pan, poaching gently until they soften. Discard the cinnamon, lightly chop the berries, add the cassis and cool completely.

Assemble three large bowls and a hand-held electric whisk. In the first bowl, place the egg yolks and half the sugar; in the second, the egg whites; in the third, the cream. Lightly whip the cream until thickened. Clean the whisks, then whisk the yolks and sugar until really pale and creamy (three or four minutes). Clean the whisks and whisk the egg whites until very soft peaks form, then add the remaining sugar slowly, continuing to whisk until thick and glossy. Gently fold all three mixtures together and tip in the cranberry mixture and its liquid. Pour into a 30 x 23 x 3.5cm tray bake tin lined with cling film and freeze. When it is hard, cut into 10 portions with the cutter (sample the offcuts!). Place on a baking tray lined with cling film, cover and freeze.

For the biscuits, preheat the oven to 180°C/fan 160°C/350°F/gas mark 4. Melt the butter, cream and sugar in a small pan over a low heat and, once the sugar dissolves, bring to the boil. Remove from the heat and fold in the pistachios, ginger, cranberries and flour. Place 10 tbsp of the mixture, each 5cm apart, across two baking trays lined with baking parchment. Flatten with a damp fork. Bake in the preheated oven for 10–12 minutes, or until golden and bubbling. Leave on the trays for a moment, then transfer to a wire rack with a palette knife. Store in an airtight container.

To serve, lay out 10 dessert plates. Put an ice on each and top with a biscuit. Decorate with cranberries and a sprig of rosemary.

christmas wreath éclairs

I always enjoyed going to one particular friend's house after school, as we would have chocolate éclairs. All these years later I bake my own. They are something else, and not too difficult to master.

These are generously sized. To make the usual shape, pipe 18 x 7cm-long éclairs. I give two glazes here; one is lighter and sweeter, aimed at children (seen on the plate with the fork in the photo).

Makes 6

50g unsalted butter, softened,
    in pieces, plus more for the
    trays (optional)
pinch of fine salt
½ tsp caster sugar
80g plain flour, sifted
2 eggs

FOR THE FILLING

250ml double cream
1 tsp vanilla extract
1 tbsp icing sugar

FOR THE DARK CHOCOLATE ICING

150g dark chocolate,
    finely chopped
1 tbsp unsalted butter
1 tbsp icing sugar

FOR THE LIGHT CHOCOLATE ICING

150g icing sugar
3 tsp cocoa
1 tsp liquid glucose

TO DECORATE

tiny gold edible stars

TOOLS

large piping bag fitted with
    1–1.5cm nozzle

Preheat the oven to 220°C/fan 200°C/425°F/gas mark 7. Line two baking trays with baking parchment, or butter two trays well.

Put the butter and 125ml of water, the salt and sugar into a pan and place over a gentle heat until melted, then increase the heat and bring to a boil. Remove from the heat and add the flour all at once, beating vigorously with a wooden spoon until the mixture pulls away from the pan. Reduce the heat to very low and beat for 30 seconds to dry the mixture a little, but not too much or the éclairs will crack in the oven. Cool for three or four minutes. Set one egg aside, place in a bowl and break it up with a fork. Crack the other egg into the mixture and beat it in. Gradually add the remaining egg, beating hard after each addition. You may not need it all. The dough will become shiny and fall from the spoon.

Spoon it into the piping bag, and pipe six 10cm diameter circles on the baking trays. Bake for 10 minutes, then reduce the oven temperature to 180°C/fan 160°C/350°F/gas mark 4 and bake for 15–20 minutes, until crisp. Slit the side of each and leave to cool.

For the filling, whip the cream to soft peaks, then add the vanilla and icing sugar. Split the éclairs in half and pipe in the cream.

For the dark icing, place a heatproof bowl over simmering water; the bowl should not touch the water. Place the chocolate, 2 tbsp of water and the butter in the bowl and melt. Sift in the icing sugar, mix and cool slightly. For the lighter icing, sift the icing sugar and cocoa into a bowl. Stir in 4–5 tsp of water and the liquid glucose, aiming for the consistency of double cream.

Spread your choice of icing over the éclairs, allow it to set slightly and finally sprinkle with stars.

upside down clementine and star anise cake

Perfect for a gathering during the festive season, this is a delicious dessert to serve warm from the oven. It's a cross between a tarte Tatin and a cake. You will need a 28cm heavy-based non-stick ovenproof frying pan to make this cake, but it's worth it, and the pan will be used for all sorts of savoury dishes too. I make no apology for including two recipes in this chapter with star anise: it's the most fabulous flavour for winter baking.

Serves 10

FOR THE TOPPING

120g unsalted butter, chilled,
   in a block
120g white caster sugar
8–10 star anise
12–15 small sweet and seedless
   clementines, peeled and halved
   horizontally

FOR THE SPONGE

175g unsalted butter, really soft,
   in pieces
175g golden caster sugar
175g self-raising flour, sifted
3 eggs, lightly beaten
finely grated zest and juice of
   2 clementines (organic
   if possible)

Preheat the oven to 180°C/fan 160°C/350°F/gas mark 4.

To make the topping, slice the butter as thinly as you can and lay flat all over the base of a 28cm heavy-based non-stick ovenproof frying pan. Sprinkle the caster sugar evenly all over the butter (these will meld to form a delicious caramel). Press the star anise (prettiest side down) into the butter, then arrange the cut halves of the clementines very tightly together all over the base of the pan (it is best to start from the outside and work inwards). The clementines need to be packed closely so they hold together when turned out later on. Have ready a sink of cold water.

Place the pan over a low heat so the butter and sugar melt and the caramel becomes pale gold. Be really careful that it doesn't become too deep brown as it will continue to cook in the oven. Stop the cooking by dipping the base of the pan into a sink of cold water. (Be careful; you don't want any water in the pan.)

Place all the ingredients for the sponge into a food mixer or food processor and blend until smooth. Pour over the clementines, spreading it to the edges. Bake in the hot oven for 20–25 minutes, until golden brown and risen; a skewer should come out clean.

Leave for a few minutes to firm up, then tip the pan upside down on to a serving plate. Remove the pan, carefully prising off and rearranging any clementines that have stuck to it. Serve warm, warning guests not to eat the star anise! It's nice with a bowl of crème fraîche, or cream flavoured with a dash of Grand Marnier.

chocolate cardamom tart

Be warned: this is very rich, very dark and it's hard to resist just another small slice. Cardamom and dark chocolate go hand in hand and the filling has no sugar, so this is a very grown-up chocolate tart with a touch of the exotic. I've decorated it with white chocolate 'snow flurries', but you could of course lightly dust it with cocoa instead. The pastry case can be assembled, then wrapped well and frozen, unbaked, if it's easier.

Serves 8–10

FOR THE CHOCOLATE PASTRY CASE

170g plain flour, plus more
    to dust

2 tbsp cocoa

pinch of salt

80g icing sugar

100g unsalted butter, in pieces,
    chilled slightly, then softened,
    plus more for the tin

1 egg yolk

FOR THE DARK CHOCOLATE FILLING

285ml double cream

seeds from 12 cardamom pods,
    ground in a mortar and pestle
    (see page 85)

200g very best 70% cocoa solids
    chocolate, very finely chopped

50g unsalted butter, in pieces

FOR THE WHITE CHOCOLATE TOPPING

50g white chocolate, finely
    chopped

Sift the flour, cocoa, salt and icing sugar into a bowl. With your fingertips, rub in the butter (or pulse in a food processor), to form crumbs. Add the egg yolk and 1–2 tbsp of ice-cold water, to make a dough. Do not over-work or it will toughen. Wrap in cling film and rest in the fridge for at least an hour. Lightly butter a 35 x 10cm loose-based tart tin.

On a floured work top, roll out the pastry to about 3mm thick and lift into the tin. Press gently around the edges (use a finger or a wooden spoon handle) and remove the excess by running the rolling pin over the tin. Prick with a fork and chill for one hour. Preheat the oven to 190°C/fan 170°C/375°F/gas mark 5 and place a baking sheet inside to heat up.

Line the pastry case with baking parchment, fill it with baking beans, raw lentils or rice and bake on the baking sheet in the preheated oven for 20 minutes. Remove the paper and beans and bake for another five to 10 minutes, ensuring the edges don't catch. If they are darkening, cover the edges with pieces of foil. Remove from the oven and cool completely.

To make the filling, place the cream and cardamom in a saucepan, bring just to the boil, then remove from the heat. Stir in the chocolate and butter until smooth, then pour into the pastry case. At the same time, melt the white chocolate in a heatproof bowl over a very gentle heat, ensuring the bowl does not touch the water. Drizzle it over the dark chocolate tart and, with the tip of a cocktail stick or point of a knife, swirl the two together. Cover and chill for a few hours to set before serving.

crumble mince pies (or squares)

Everyone likes these. They can be assembled well ahead of Christmas, frozen and freshly baked to serve. Ideally, try to use home-made mincemeat (see Fig and Almond Mincemeat, overleaf), draining it of excess liquid. If you use a bought jar of mincemeat, improve it with a splash of brandy.

Makes 24 pies or squares

250g unsalted butter, chilled, in
    pieces, plus more for the trays

250g plain flour, plus more
    to dust

pinch of salt

125g ground almonds

finely grated zest of 1 large
    unwaxed lemon and 1 large
    organic orange

100g caster sugar

600g mincemeat

50g flaked almonds

icing sugar, to dust (optional)

TOOLS

7cm circle cutter (if making
    mince pies)

Butter two 12-hole bun trays or a 33 x 22cm tray bake tin very well. (Or you can use a silicone tray prepared according to the manufacturer's instructions.) Dust the holes in the bun trays with flour, tapping out excess, or line the base and sides of the tray bake tin with baking parchment.

In a large bowl, or a food processor, sift the flour and salt and add the ground almonds, lemon and orange zests, sugar and butter. Rub it in with your fingertips, or blitz in the processor, until it just resembles crumbs. Remove 200g of the mixture, cover and set aside. Blend the rest together until it just forms a ball. Do not over-mix. Wrap in cling film and chill for an hour. When ready to bake, preheat the oven to 190°C/fan 170°C/375°F/gas mark 5.

On a well-floured work top, roll out the pastry to about 3mm thick. If making pies, stamp out 24 circles with the cutter and press lightly into the holes in the trays. If making squares, roll the pastry out to a rectangle and press into the tin. Spoon the mincemeat between the holes, or into the tin. Sprinkle over the reserved crumble and the flaked almonds. (At this point you can freeze them, and defrost when ready to bake.)

Bake the pies in the preheated oven for 20–25 minutes, or the tray bake for 35–40 minutes, or until golden brown. Leave the pies for 20 minutes to firm up in the trays, then very gently remove to a wire rack. Leave the tray bake to cool completely, then cut into squares. Serve dusted with icing sugar, if you like.

fig and almond mincemeat

So very simple to make and even more delicious when made a good month or two ahead of Christmas. Use the very best-quality ingredients you can find.

Makes 1.25kg

100g whole almonds

250g Bramley apples, peeled, cored and finely chopped

200g raisins (Lexia or Muscatel if you can find them)

150g currants

150g dried figs, finely chopped

100g suet (beef or vegetable)

100g whole mixed peel, finely snipped with scissors

100g demerara sugar

100g dark muscovado sugar

30ml brandy or rum, or 60ml if not using amaretto

30ml amaretto (optional)

finely grated zest and juice of 1 large unwaxed lemon and 1 large organic orange

1½ tsp mixed spice

1 tsp ground cinnamon

Preheat the oven to 180°C/fan 160°C/350°F/gas mark 4. Put the almonds on a baking tray and cook for five minutes, turning once, until lightly toasted. Remove, cool slightly and chop.

Stir all the ingredients together in a large mixing bowl. Cover the bowl and set aside for up to 24 hours for the flavours to mingle, stirring every now and then. Pack the mincemeat into sterilised jars (see page 27) and seal. Stored in a cool dark place, the mincemeat will keep for 12 months or more.

spicy cheese biscuits

I always have at least one of these cheese biscuit dough logs in my freezer, ready to slice thinly and bake to serve with festive drinks. Baked and wrapped in little bags, they also make a lovely gift. You can ring the changes with these biscuits, using stilton cheese with about 50g of very finely chopped walnuts to coat, or gruyère cheese with sesame seeds, instead of the parmesan and poppy seeds.

Makes 1 log / 30–36 biscuits

85g finely grated parmesan
    cheese

85g plain flour, sifted

pinch of salt

pinch or two of cayenne pepper
    or chilli powder

80g unsalted butter, chilled, in
    pieces, plus more for the tray

1 tbsp olive oil, plus more
    if needed

2 tbsp poppy seeds

In a large bowl, mix the cheese, flour, salt and cayenne. Mix in the butter and olive oil and, with your fingertips, gently work everything together. If it is too crumbly, add a drop more olive oil.

Place the poppy seeds on a small tray or plate.

Roll the dough into a log shape, about 20cm long, then roll it in the poppy seeds. Wrap in cling film and chill for 30 minutes. (Or wrap and freeze until needed. Defrost before continuing to bake the biscuits.) When ready to bake, preheat the oven to 180°C/fan 160°C/350°F/gas mark 4 and butter a baking tray.

Cut the log into 30–36 thin slices and place on the tray. Bake in the preheated oven for 10–15 minutes. They will be a beautiful golden colour and smell divine, though are quite fragile, so handle them carefully. Cool on a wire rack… and just try to resist!

fig, port and star anise christmas cake

All the flavours of Christmas combine in this deliciously moreish cake; make it up to a few months ahead for the best flavour. It's one for those who would rather forego marzipan and icing, and is to be eaten in slivers at any time, with a glass of port and a slice of Lancashire cheese.

Be sure to use the very best quality ready-to-eat dried fruits that you can afford.

Makes 25 slices

140ml port, plus 2–3 tbsp
   to feed the cake

3 star anise

500g dried figs, roughly chopped

300g dates, roughly chopped

300g prunes, roughly chopped

3 tbsp treacle

finely grated zest of 1 organic
   orange and 1 unwaxed lemon

1 tbsp mixed spice

½ tsp freshly grated nutmeg

250g unsalted butter, really soft,
   plus more for the tin

200g pecan nuts

100g hazelnuts

160g dark muscovado sugar

6 eggs, lightly beaten

170g self-raising flour, sifted

1 tsp salt

TO DECORATE

4 tbsp apricot jam

2 tbsp brandy

9 dried figs, 22 dates, 20 prunes,
   22 pecans and 5 star anise

1 egg white

pot of gold edible glitter

TOOLS

paintbrush

ribbon, or lengths of raffia

The day before making the cake, pour the port into a pan with the star anise. Bring to the boil, remove from the heat and leave for a good few hours to infuse. Place the figs, dates and prunes in a large bowl with the treacle, zests, mixed spice, nutmeg and port (removing the star anise). Stir, cover and leave overnight.

The next day, butter and line the sides and base of 23cm square, 7.5cm deep tin (do not use a loose-based tin) with baking parchment. Wrap brown paper round the tin and tie with string. Preheat the oven to 150°C/fan 130°C/300°F/gas mark 2. Put the nuts on a baking tray and cook for 10 minutes, until toasted. Cool and chop. Place a tray of hot water (large enough to hold the cake tin) in the oven. In a food mixer, beat the butter and sugar for at least five minutes, until pale and creamy. Mix in the eggs slowly, adding 1 tbsp of flour to stop the mixture curdling. Using a large spoon, fold in the remaining flour, the salt, the fruits and their liquid, and the nuts. Fold together and tip into the tin.

Place in the water-filled tray and bake for 2–2½ hours, or until a skewer comes out almost clean with a couple of crumbs on it. If the top is browning before it is cooked, protect with foil (see page 50). Cool in the tin, on a wire rack. When cold, prick all over with a skewer and sprinkle over the extra port. Wrap in baking parchment and then in foil, and leave for at least a few weeks.

A week before Christmas, bring the jam and brandy to the boil, push through a sieve and brush most of it over the cake. Decorate with dried fruits and nuts, glazing with more jam. Paint the star anise with egg white and glitter, and add (they are not for eating). Wrap the sides of the cake with baking parchment or clear film to stop it drying out. Finish with a ribbon or lengths of raffia.

chocolate roulade

Somehow Christmas wouldn't be complete without a chocolate roulade. Everyone loves it. It can be made 24 hours ahead, or even frozen, but is best filled only a few hours before you need it. You can fill it in a variety of ways; I've given several suggestions.

Serves 8

FOR THE ROULADE

unsalted butter, for the tin

180g 60–70% cocoa solids chocolate, chopped

5 eggs

150g golden caster sugar

1 tbsp cocoa, sifted

icing sugar, to dust

FOR A CREAM FILLING

300ml double cream, lightly whipped

1 tbsp icing sugar

OPTIONAL ADDITIONS

- **mix the cream** with 1 tbsp rum or brandy
- **top the cream** with 150g chestnut purée
- **top the cream** with well-drained chopped canned pears
- **top the cream** with well-drained canned morello cherries

FOR A WHITE CHOCOLATE GANACHE FILLING

150g good-quality white chocolate, very finely chopped

150ml double cream

Preheat the oven to 180°C/fan 160°C/350°F/gas mark 4. Lightly butter a Swiss roll tin and line the base and sides snugly with baking parchment. Melt the chocolate in a small heatproof bowl over a pan of gently simmering water, ensuring the bowl does not touch the water. Set aside (but keep the pan on the hob).

Break the eggs into a larger heatproof bowl, tip in the sugar and place the bowl on top of the pan of simmering water, ensuring the bowl does not touch the water. Using a hand-held electric whisk, beat for five minutes, until thick and pale. Remove from the heat. Pour in the chocolate and cocoa and fold together. Pour into the prepared tin and bake in the preheated oven for 15–20 minutes, or until the roulade has firmed up but is still moist. Cover with baking parchment and a clean tea towel and leave to cool (it can be made the day before). It will shrink a little.

When ready to assemble, place a new sheet of baking parchment on the work top and dust liberally with icing sugar. Turn the roulade out on to the icing sugar and remove the top paper. If using a cream filling, mix the cream with the icing sugar and rum, if using, and, using a palette knife, spread it all over the roulade, stopping 2–3cm short of the long side furthest from you. If adding one of the toppings, spread it over the cream.

Or, to make the white chocolate ganache, place the chocolate in a bowl and bring the cream to the boil. Pour the cream over the chocolate, leave it for a few minutes, then gently stir until smooth. Leave until cold, chill for a few hours, then whip until it thickens. Spread the white chocolate ganache over the roulade as above.

Starting at the long side nearest you (using the paper to help) roll up the roulade fairly tightly. The cake will crack slightly, but this is normal. Give it a snowy fall of icing sugar just before serving.

sparkling iced igloo

If a rich and flaming Christmas pudding is not your thing – or you have younger mouths to feed – this igloo, hiding a treasure of chocolate coins, is perfect. It can be made days in advance. The secret is to make all the components ahead and, when ready to serve, decorate and get straight to the table.

Serves 8

FOR THE MINT ICE CREAM

750ml double cream

5 egg yolks, at room temperature

220g caster sugar

pinch of salt

1 tsp vanilla extract

1 tsp peppermint extract

OR

1 litre good-quality shop-
   bought vanilla ice cream

1 tsp peppermint extract

FOR THE IGLOO

20 mint Matchmakers, chopped

3 chocolate coins (foil removed)

30–40g desiccated coconut

2 x 150g packets of clear mints

Place the cream in a pan and bring to the boil. In a large bowl using a hand-held electric whisk (or in a food mixer), whisk the egg yolks and sugar until really thick and creamy; three or four minutes. Pour the cream slowly over the egg yolks, still whisking, and beat in the salt, vanilla and peppermint extracts. Cool, then chill. When cold, if you have an ice cream machine, churn it. If not, place in a container with a lid and freeze for an hour or two, then whisk and refreeze. Repeat a couple of times. If using shop-bought ice cream, let soften, then mix in the peppermint extract.

Whichever way you made it, mix in the Matchmakers and tip into a one-litre freezer-proof bowl. Freeze until semi-frozen, then bury the chocolate coins in it. Freeze solid. To remove from the bowl, dip it into a sink of hot water and run a knife around the edge. Turn out on to the thin cake board (it should be cut to fit the base of the dome) and sprinkle with coconut. It can now stay in the freezer for a few days ready to be served.

FOR THE PENGUIN FAMILY

150g white sugarpaste

black food colour paste

tube of white royal icing

tube of black royal icing

orange food colour paste

red food colour paste

pot of Sugarflair edible pearl
   white lustre, or edible
   clear glitter

TOOLS

round thin cake board

35cm round silver cake drum

You can make the penguins in advance and store in a box, not an airtight container or the fridge. Mine are 6cm, 4cm and 2cm high. To make a penguin, form a cone from white sugarpaste. Colour a little sugarpaste with black food colour (see page 62) and roll to 3mm thick. Cut out a heart shape, to fold around the back of the penguin to form wings; the tip of the heart is at the top of his head. Use white royal icing to stick together. Pipe the eyes using black royal icing and colour tiny pieces of sugarpaste orange for beaks and red for a hat (see page 62). Attach using white royal icing and add a white pom-pom to the hat. Roll white snowballs. For the ice, place the mints in a bag and smash with a rolling pin.

To serve, place the dome on the drum. Stick on a snowball 'door' with royal icing. Arrange the ice and penguins around and sprinkle with lustre or glitter. Bring to the table and await the applause!

cranberry and amaretto stollen cake

My friend Jacqui created this delicious cake by taking some of the elements of the German sweet bread stollen — such as the fruited moist crumb and marzipan centre — and turning it into a cake. It's packed with cranberries laced with amaretto and given a hint of spice and orange... slightly unusual flavours for a stollen, but utterly delicious. Make this at least a day before you want to eat it.

Serves 12

FOR THE CAKE

150g dried cranberries

100ml amaretto

½ tsp freshly grated nutmeg

½ tsp freshly ground cardamom
  seeds (see page 85)

finely grated zest of 1 organic
  orange and juice of ½

120g unsalted butter, really soft,
  in pieces, plus more for the tin

about 200g very good-quality
  shop-bought marzipan, or
  home-made (see page 50;
  make just ½ the recipe)

350g white spelt flour
  (or plain flour)

2 tsp baking powder

pinch of salt

120g golden caster sugar

200ml crème fraîche

2 eggs, lightly beaten

100g ground almonds

FOR THE TOPPING

40g unsalted butter, melted

1–1½ tbsp amaretto

First of all (and the night before if you can) place the cranberries, amaretto, nutmeg, cardamom and orange zest and juice in a bowl, stir, then leave for at least a few hours.

Butter a 30 x 10 x 10cm loaf tin and line with baking parchment. Preheat the oven to 190°C/fan 170°C/375°F/gas mark 5.

Roll the marzipan into a log about 2.5cm in diameter and 3–4cm shorter than the tin.

To make the cake, sift together the flour, baking powder and salt and set aside. Place the butter and sugar in a food mixer (or use a large bowl and a hand-held electric whisk) and cream together for four or five minutes, until light and creamy. Add the crème fraîche and mix. Continuing to whisk, slowly add the eggs, tipping in 1 tbsp of the flour mixture to stop it curdling. Fold in the remaining flour, ground almonds, cranberry mixture and every drop of liquid.

Tip half the batter into the prepared tin, lay the marzipan roll right down the centre, slightly pressing it down, then cover with the remaining mix. Smooth the top and bake for 45–55 minutes. Test with a skewer down the sides (not the middle because of the marzipan). It will probably be slightly cracked on top; this is fine.

Meanwhile, mix the melted butter and amaretto together and, as soon as the cake comes out of the oven, prick the surface all over with a cocktail stick. Brush the amaretto butter all over the top and leave in the tin to firm up for 20–30 minutes. Tip out to cool completely (top uppermost) on a wire rack. When cold, wrap well in baking parchment and then in foil. Serve the cake after at least a day, though it keeps very well for several days.

a dozen christmas shortbreads

Take one simple, delicious, buttery shortbread recipe and transform it very easily into a whole array of flavours and shapes. Of course, don't keep these just for Christmas, everyone loves freshly baked shortbread all through the year. Maybe just put away the Christmas tree cutter, though…

Use your own imagination to create your very own flavours and shapes, the possibilities are endless. Packed into little boxes or bags they make a lovely gift and, in my experience, will always be very gratefully received.

The uncooked shortbread dough freezes brilliantly so you can make and cut them out weeks ahead, lay them between sheets of baking parchment in a freezer container, and freeze; defrost and freshly bake as required. All the baked shortbreads do store in an airtight tin for a week or so (except for the Caramel Sandwiches and the Glazed Clementine and Cardamom Rounds as they will go soft after a day or two). But for all shortbreads, just cooled and straight out of the oven — as my family will tell you — is when they are at their very best. They will disappear rapidly.

The exact quantities and the baking times will of course vary slightly, depending on the size and thickness of the shortbreads.

Makes about 20

125g salted butter, softened, in pieces

50g golden caster sugar, plus more to sprinkle (do not sprinkle any of the other shortbreads with sugar after baking)

125g plain flour, plus more to dust

60g cornflour

TOOLS

4.5cm round fluted cutter

CLASSIC BASIC SHORTBREAD RECIPE

Line a baking tray with baking parchment.

Place the butter and sugar in the bowl of a food mixer (or use a bowl and a hand-held electric whisk). Cream the butter and sugar, then gradually sift in the flour and cornflour, mixing as you do, just until everything is blended. Do not over-mix. Wrap in cling film and chill for 20–30 minutes, to make it easier to handle.

On a lightly floured work top, roll the dough out to about 5mm thick and, using the round fluted cutter, stamp out the shortbreads as closely together as you can. Gather the scraps and re-roll them. (The fewer times you re-roll the dough the better, as it will toughen it.) Lay the shortbreads on the prepared baking tray and chill for 20–30 minutes (so they will hold their shapes better). Preheat the oven to 180°C/fan 160°C/350°F/gas mark 4. Bake the shortbreads in the preheated oven for 15–20 minutes. Sprinkle with caster sugar and leave to cool on the tray.

VANILLA CHRISTMAS TREES

Add 1 tsp vanilla extract (or the seeds from one-third of a vanilla pod) when creaming the butter and sugar. Cut out 7cm Christmas trees with a cutter and press six or seven multicoloured dragees (for baubles) on to each tree. Chill and bake as before.

CRANBERRY COCONUT SNOWBALLS

Add 1 tsp vanilla extract when creaming the butter and sugar. With the flour, add 30g dried cranberries, roughly chopped. Roll into 20 equal-sized balls. Chill and bake as before.

Melt 200g of white chocolate. Hold a ball on a fork and spoon it over, then set the balls on a wire rack with baking parchment underneath. Sprinkle with 60g of desiccated coconut.

VERY LEMONY FINGERS

Add the finely grated zest of 1 large unwaxed lemon when creaming the butter and sugar. Roll out, then cut into 20 shortbread fingers, each 7 x 2cm. Chill and bake as before.

When cold, make a lemon icing: mix 50g of icing sugar with the juice of ¼–½ lemon. Dip each finger into the icing. Leave to set on a tray lined with baking parchment.

WALNUT AND CINNAMON SQUARES

Lightly roast 30g of walnuts in the oven for five minutes. Cool, finely chop and add with the flour and 1 tsp ground cinnamon. Cut into 4.5cm squares. Prick each three or four times with a fork. Chill and bake as before.

ALMOND SLICES

Lightly roast 30g of nibbed almonds in the oven for four minutes. Cool and fold in with the flour. Cut the dough into 20 fingers, each 7 x 2cm. Press a whole blanched almond into the top of each. Chill and bake as before.

CARAMEL SANDWICHES

Roll out the shortbread dough to about 3mm thick and, using a 4.5cm round cutter, stamp out about 36 rounds. Cut a 1.5cm star (or round shape) from the centre of half of them. Chill as before. Bake for around 15 minutes and, once cold, sandwich one solid circle and one with a hole cut out together, using ½ tsp of dulce de leche or caramel spread. Repeat to fill all the shortbreads. Once filled, these are best eaten within a day as the caramel will soon turn them soft.

CHERRY SQUARES

Add 80g red glacé cherries (rinsed, dried and roughly chopped) with the flour. Cut into 4.5cm squares. Chill and bake as before.

GLAZED CLEMENTINE AND CARDAMOM ROUNDS

Add ½ tsp freshly ground cardamom (see page 85) with the flour. Using a 4.5cm cutter, stamp out 20 rounds. Chill as before. When the shortbreads are on the tray, top each with a very thin slice of clementine, dried very well with kitchen paper. Bake for 20–22 minutes. Sprinkle over 2–3 tbsp of caster sugar as soon as they come out of the oven and leave to cool. Remove the baking parchment from under the shortbreads. Using a blowtorch, glaze each clementine slice. The star shape of the cut clementine will be highlighted. These are best eaten within two days, as they will soften.

CHOCOLATE PINWHEELS

Make the classic shortbread recipe as usual. Now make a second batch, but using only 100g of flour and adding 25g of cocoa.

Roll the chocolate dough into a 3mm-thick rectangle about 26 x 18cm. Repeat with the vanilla dough. Lay one on top of the other and trim the sides neatly. Carefully lift on to a sheet of baking parchment with a long side towards you. Use the paper to help roll the dough into a log. Chill as before, then cut into 40 discs about 5mm thick. Bake for about 20 minutes.

CHOCOLATE CHILLI HEARTS

Reduce the plain flour to 100g and add 25g cocoa and ½–1 finely chopped red chilli (to taste) with the flour. Roll out to 3mm thick. Cut out 40 shortbreads with a 4.5cm heart cutter. Chill and bake as before.

ORANGE-GLAZED GINGER STARS

Add 1 tsp ground ginger and 1 large ball of finely chopped stem ginger with the flour. Cut out with a 4.5cm star cutter. Chill and bake as before.

When cold, make an orange glaze by mixing 100g of sifted icing sugar and the juice of ½–1 orange and dip or ice each star. Scatter with sprinkles and leave to set.

rosemary roasted nuts

I have been asked for this recipe more times than I can remember. I make them all year round, but they seem especially appropriate at Christmas when I make a double batch (at least). Store them in a Kilner jar ready to be lightly warmed through and served with drinks. Packed into such a jar, or into little cellophane bags tied with a ribbon, they make a wonderful gift too.

Makes about 450g

70g unsalted butter, in pieces

2 tbsp dark muscovado sugar

large pinch of cayenne pepper,
   or more to taste

1 tsp sea salt

large sprig of rosemary, needles
   removed and finely chopped

finely grated zest of 1 organic
   orange

400g mixed whole nuts, such as
   hazelnuts and almonds, and
   pecan and walnut halves

Preheat the oven to 180°C/fan 160°C/350°F/gas mark 4. Melt the butter and sugar in a pan. Add the cayenne, salt, rosemary and orange zest. Stir well and tip in the nuts. Stir to coat well and pour on to a baking tray, spreading them out in a single layer. Roast in the preheated oven for about 12 minutes (watch they don't catch). Cool on the tray and, when cold, pack into a storage jar, or an airtight container.

To serve, gently warm through for a few minutes.

santa is on his way!

Santa, Rudolph and his reindeer are coming, laden with edible goodies! A wonderful Christmas gift.

Makes 12

FOR THE CAKES

grated zest and juice of 1 orange

40g sultanas

180g self-raising flour

1 tsp baking powder

2–3 tsp ground cinnamon

pinch of salt

180g unsalted butter, really soft

120g golden caster sugar

1 tsp vanilla extract

3 eggs, lightly beaten

100g dulce de leche

FOR THE ORANGE BUTTERCREAM

220g unsalted butter, softened

finely grated zest of 2 oranges

300g icing sugar, sifted

2–3 tbsp milk

TO DECORATE

500g light brown sugarpaste

Matchmakers chocolates

chocolate buttons and beans

60g bag white royal icing

150g red sugarpaste

pot of edible glue

tiny edible stocking fillers!

30g white sugarpaste

pot of edible pearl white lustre

liquorice pin wheel

pot of white sugar crystals

TOOLS

9cm round cutter

paintbrush

Preheat the oven to 180°C/fan 160°C/350°F/gas mark 4. Line a cupcake tray with 12 cases, three red for Santa and his parcels and nine brown for the reindeer. Place the orange zest, juice and sultanas in a bowl for 30 minutes for the sultanas to plump up.

Sift the flour, baking powder, cinnamon and salt into a bowl. With a hand-held electric whisk, blend in the butter, sugar, vanilla and eggs. Fold in the dulce de leche, sultanas and orange juice. Divide between the cases and bake for 15–20 minutes, until they spring back to the touch. Leave in the tray for a few minutes, then cool on a wire rack. For the buttercream, beat the butter and orange zest until paler. Add the icing sugar and beat for five minutes. Mix in the milk. Using a palette knife, cover the cakes, doming the buttercream on the nine in brown cases (for reindeer noses).

On a work top dusted with icing sugar, roll out brown sugarpaste to 3–4mm thick. Stamp out nine discs with the cutter and place over each cake in a brown case, moulding it slightly over the case. For the antlers, snap a few Matchmakers and press in. Attach a chocolate nose and eyes with royal icing. (Make Rudolph's nose from red sugarpaste and paint on a shine with edible glue.)

Roll out the red sugarpaste and cut out three discs. Cover as for the reindeer, but slightly dome Santa's body by placing a little red sugarpaste under the disc. Stick on the edible gifts to two of the red cakes, using royal icing, to form the sacks of presents.

Create Santa's head and nose by mixing white and red sugarpaste. Mould the white beard and moustache from white sugarpaste and sprinkle with lustre. Use the royal icing to attach the head, beard, moustache and nose, and edible glue to attach two tiny liquorice eyes and a liquorice 'belt'. Mould a hat from red and white sugarpaste, sticking on sugar crystals with royal icing to create the 'fur'. Santa, Rudolph and his reindeer are now ready; sure to bring delight wherever they go!

gilded (or not) gingerbread men

Years ago I visited the Shopes, an elderly couple who lived in a wonderful house they had designed and built in the middle of a wood in Connecticut. Mrs Shope was known for her baking, and one of her specialities was her gingerbread, which she made in huge batches to give away at Christmas. Here is her recipe, which her daughter Chrissie has kindly given to me.

To this American gingerbread I am adding a very British finishing touch. Gilded gingerbreads were made as early as Tudor times: from simple biscuits to huge, exotic, moulded affairs shaped as Kings and Queens with golden crowns. They were called fairings, and sold at country fairs all over England. By gilding your gingerbread men and offering them as a gift, you will be continuing one of our oldest traditions, which I think makes a very special (and extravagant) gift at Christmas.

Makes 20–25

FOR THE GINGERBREAD

300g plain flour, plus more to dust

1 tsp ground ginger

1 tsp ground cinnamon

½ tsp bicarbonate of soda

120g unsalted butter, in pieces

140g treacle

120g light muscovado sugar

1 tbsp white wine vinegar

1 egg, lightly beaten

TO DECORATE

60g bag white royal icing, no. 1 nozzle

few sheets of pure gold leaf

TOOLS

9cm gingerbread man cutter

paintbrush

In a large bowl, sift together the flour, spices and bicarbonate of soda and set aside. Place the butter, treacle, sugar and vinegar in a heavy-based pan and bring to a rolling boil. Allow to cool to blood temperature, then tip in the dry ingredients and mix well, adding the egg as you do. Wrap in cling film and chill overnight (or for at least two hours) to firm up.

Line two trays with baking parchment. On a lightly floured work top, roll out the dough to 3–4mm thick and cut out the gingerbread men using the cutter, as closely as you can. Place on the prepared trays and re-roll to use all the dough. At this point you can freeze the biscuits. Chill for 30 minutes. Preheat the oven to 190°C/fan 170°C/375°F/gas mark 5, then bake in the oven for eight to 10 minutes; they will darken. Leave to cool on the trays. They will harden and your kitchen will fill with a delicious aroma.

Once cold, decorate the gingerbreads. I piped some and gilded others, the choice is yours. Using the royal icing, pipe two eyes, a nose and a mouth, then add patterns as you choose.

To gild the gingerbread completely, lay a sheet of gold leaf over a gingerbread on the tray, smoothing it gently with a paintbrush. To gild them partly, use the tip of a fine paintbrush to apply specks of gold leaf randomly over the gingerbread men.

a box of baubles

We have quite an assortment of Christmas tree decorations. I've kept them all, from the sequinned felt trees and stars my children made at kindergarten, to the fragile ones my daughter brought back from a German market, packed in her socks, to vintage Russian hand-painted fire cones in their original box. Our tree is full of memories, all the decorations carefully unpacked each year. You might correctly assume I have something of an obsession! So, naturally, I thought of edible baubles.

Makes 24

FOR THE CAKES

140g self-raising flour

1 tsp baking powder

1 tsp ground cinnamon

½ tsp mixed spice

½ tsp salt

175g unsalted butter, soft, diced

175g light muscovado sugar

3 eggs, lightly beaten

60g ground almonds

150g mincemeat

TO ICE AND DECORATE

4 tbsp apricot jam

500g marzipan

icing sugar, to dust

1 tbsp sherry, or boiled water

750g white sugarpaste

packet of Polo mints

60g bag white royal icing,
    no. 1 nozzle

30–50g red sugarpaste

60g bag red royal icing,
    no. 1 nozzle

TOOLS

6.5cm round cutter

7cm round cutter

selection of tiny cutters

lengths of 5mm-wide ribbon

Preheat the oven to 180°C/fan 160°C/350°F/gas mark 4. Line two fairy cake tins with red paper cases. Sift the flour into a large bowl with the baking powder, cinnamon, mixed spice and salt. Tip in the butter, sugar, eggs and almonds. Beat with a hand-held electric whisk, but don't over-mix. Fold in the mincemeat. Divide the batter between the cases and bake for 15–18 minutes, or until the cakes spring back to the touch. Leave in their tins for a minute or two, then cool on a wire rack. (You can freeze them now.)

Lay out all the cakes in front of you. Warm the jam slightly, push it through a sieve, then brush it lightly over each cake.

Roll the marzipan out to 4–5mm thick on a work top dusted with icing sugar. Using the smaller round cutter (it should measure the same as the top of the cakes), stamp out discs of marzipan and lay on top of each cake. Smooth to the edge. Repeat until all are covered. Brush lightly with sherry or cooled, boiled water. Repeat with the white sugarpaste, cutting out with the larger cutter (it should measure the same as the top of the cases) and smoothing it over the edges so the cakes are slightly domed. Press a mint into each, attaching with royal icing if needed. Leave overnight.

You can make the sugarpaste decorations in advance and store in a box, not in an airtight container or the fridge. To make the red sugarpaste decorations, roll out to about 2–3mm thick on a board dusted with icing sugar and cut out as you choose. To make buttons, cut out tiny rounds, indent the edge with a smaller cutter and make two holes with a cocktail stick. Attach all the sugarpaste decorations with royal icing. Pipe details with the white and red royal icing. Finally, thread the ribbon through the mints.

a few simple packaging ideas

One Christmas long, long ago when I was an art student (and the idea of making cakes for a living had not entered my head), I decided to package a few of my home-made shortbreads as gifts. I just couldn't understand the complete delight my simple little offerings received. Now I make beautifully packaged delicious gifts all year round. Set aside a few very pleasurable hours and bake a selection of goodies. If you plan ahead and gather a few cellophane bags, boxes, ribbons, jars and labels as you see them throughout the year, it will be so easy. You too will be completely amazed how very gratefully your edible gifts will be received.

TOOLS

selection of jars
selection of cellophane bags
selection of boxes
coloured plastic tubes and tissue paper
gift tags and sticky labels
coloured and metallic pens
lengths of ribbon and twine
little baubles or artificial berries
sprigs of rosemary, and ivy and holly leaves

RECIPES

A Box of Baubles (see page 238)
A Dozen Christmas Shortbreads
  (see page 226)
'Christmas Pudding' No Bake Cakes
  (see page 242)
Gilded (or not) Gingerbread Men
  (see page 235)
Ginger Florentines (see page 249)
Mini Christmas Fruit Cakes (see page 247)
Rosemary Roasted Nuts (see page 231)
Sloe Gin (see page 172)
Spicy Cheese Biscuits (see page 212)

OTHER IDEAS (NOT ILLUSTRATED)

Crumble Mince Pies (see page 209)
Fig, Port and Star Anise Christmas Cake
  (see page 214)

MERRY CHRISTMAS

'christmas pudding' no-bake cakes

Our traditional Christmas pudding is not for everyone – especially small children – but these little novelty chocolate Christmas puddings are a guaranteed success. Fun for the kids to make, no baking required and a lovely gift, too. If you prefer, you can make this recipe as cake 'pops', first piercing each ball with a lolly stick dipped in the white chocolate.

Makes 30

30g green sugarpaste

icing sugar, to dust

300g 50% cocoa solids
   chocolate, roughly chopped

200g plain biscuits, such as
   rich tea or digestive

2 x 40g honeycomb-centre
   chocolate bars

2 tbsp golden syrup

100g red glacé cherries, rinsed,
   dried and chopped, or dried
   cranberries

TO DECORATE

150g white chocolate, chopped

pot of red sugar pearls

TOOLS

tiny holly leaf cutter

The holly leaves can be made several weeks in advance: roll out the green sugarpaste to about 2mm thick on a work top dusted with icing sugar and cut out 60 leaves with the cutter. Score a line down the centre of each. Keep in a cardboard box until needed (not in an airtight container or in the fridge, or they will 'sweat').

When ready to make the Christmas puddings, put the chocolate into a heatproof bowl and stand it over gently simmering water, ensuring the bowl does not touch the water. Place the biscuits in a polythene bag and, holding the end tight, bash them with a rolling pin to crumbs. Crush the honeycomb bars in the same way, but keep them as slightly larger chunks.

Once the chocolate has melted, take it off the heat and cool slightly. Stir in the crushed biscuits, honeycomb bars, syrup and cherries or cranberries. Stir everything together well. Roll into about 30 balls and place into 30 petits fours cases.

Melt the white chocolate in a small heatproof bowl standing over barely simmering water (ensuring the bowl does not touch the water). Take off the heat and cool slightly.

Using a teaspoon, drizzle a little white chocolate on each little Christmas pudding and, while still wet, top with the holly leaves and red sugar pearls. Leave to dry, then eat them up within a few days (shouldn't be too hard…).

christmas roses and mistletoe cake

This is a traditional fruit cake but with chocolate; make it at least one week ahead. Alternatively, or as well, make mini fruit cakes by cutting it into rounds (see page 247). If making decorations in advance, you can make enough for both the large and mini cakes with 250g of sugarpaste.

Makes about 20 slices

FOR THE CHOCOLATE FRUIT CAKE

170g sultanas

170g raisins, preferably Lexia
   or Muscatel

60g currants

60g glacé ginger, finely chopped

finely grated zest of 2 organic
   oranges

200g golden syrup

4 tbsp sherry (I like to use
   amontillado), plus 2 tbsp
   to feed the cake

150g unsalted butter, softened,
   in pieces, plus more for the tin

50g 70% cocoa solids chocolate,
   chopped

100g self-raising flour

2 tbsp cocoa

½ tsp salt

60g blanched almonds, chopped

150g dark muscovado sugar

3 eggs, lightly beaten

60g ground almonds

130g undyed glacé cherries,
   rinsed, dried and halved

The day before, place the sultanas, raisins, currants, ginger, orange zest, golden syrup and sherry in a bowl, stir well, cover with cling film and leave overnight.

Preheat the oven to 150°C/fan 130°C/300°F/gas mark 2. Lightly butter a 23cm diameter, 7.5cm deep round tin and line with baking parchment. Wrap brown paper (or newspaper) round the outside and tie with string. This will help the cake stay moist.

Melt the chocolate in a heatproof bowl set over a pan of simmering water, ensuring the bowl does not touch the water. Leave to cool. Sift together the flour, cocoa and salt and set aside. Place the blanched almonds on a baking tray and roast in the preheated oven for seven or eight minutes. Set these aside too.

In the bowl of a food mixer (or a bowl using a hand-held electric whisk), cream together the butter and sugar for four or five minutes, until light and fluffy. On a slow speed, gradually add the eggs, mixing well and alternating with a spoonful of the flour mixture. Do not over-mix. Once all the egg is combined, fold in the remaining flour mixture and ground almonds. Finally tip in the fruits, including every drop of liquid, the glacé cherries, nuts and melted chocolate. Fold well together and tip into the tin.

Smooth the surface of the cake and bake for 2–2½ hours, or until a skewer comes out clean. If it starts to brown too much on the surface, cut a circle of foil slightly larger than the cake tin, tear the centre open and place over the tin; this will protect the sides.

Remove the cake from the oven and cool in the tin. When it is cold, prick with a fine skewer and sprinkle over the extra sherry. Wrap well in baking parchment, then in foil and leave to mature for a week or two, or up to a couple of months.

4 tbsp apricot jam, warmed
    and pressed through a sieve

1kg marzipan

icing sugar, to dust

1 tbsp sherry, or cooled
    boiled water

1.25kg off-white/cream
    sugarpaste

edible gold sparkle lustre

Sugarflair food colour pastes
    in Eucalyptus and
    Christmas Green

pot of Sugarflair edible pearl
    white lustre

packet of flower paste (see page
    252 for suppliers)

white vegetable fat, if needed

60g bag white royal icing,
    (or pot of edible glue)

TOOLS

25cm round cake drum

Jem tool no. 9 (optional)

1.5cm mini calyx cutter

set of PME plunger ivy cutters
    (small and medium)

paintbrushes

set of PME plunger holly cutters
    (small and medium, see page
    252 for suppliers)

2 metal mistletoe leaf cutters
    (4cm and 5cm)

boning tool (optional)

3.5cm PME petal cutter

ball tool

small piece of fine netting

1m 3.5cm-wide ribbon

double-sided sticky tape
    (optional)

Dab a little jam on the cake drum and place the cake on it upside down. If there are any holes, fill them with bits of marzipan. Brush all over with jam. Knead the marzipan until pliable. Dust a work top with icing sugar and roll the marzipan out 5mm thick, in a circle slightly larger than the top and sides of the cake. Lift on to the cake, smooth with your hands and cut away the excess. Leave to firm up overnight. Brush the marzipan all over with the sherry. Roll out and apply 1kg of the sugarpaste as with the marzipan. Leave overnight.

The decorations can be made months in advance and stored in a box (not in an airtight container or the fridge, or they will 'sweat'). To make golden berries, take a small amount of sugarpaste and roll it into 12 pea-sized balls. Indent with the Jem tool to form a tiny star, if using. Place gold lustre into a dish and roll them in it. Leave to dry. Make the calyx centres for the Christmas roses by rolling out a small piece of sugarpaste to 2mm thick. Cut out 12 with the mini calyx cutter. Next colour the remaining sugarpaste two or three shades of soft green, using the food colour pastes (see page 62). To make the ivy leaves, roll out the darkest green sugarpaste to 2mm thick. Stamp out with the cutters. Tweak slightly so the leaves are not flat and paint with the pearl lustre. The holly leaves are made in the same way, with the holly cutters. To make the mistletoe leaves roll out pale green sugarpaste to 2mm thick. Cut out with the cutters. Using a boning tool, or the handle of a teaspoon, stroke the leaf so it curls slightly and, with a sharp knife, draw a line down the centre. Allow all the leaves to dry.

For the Christmas roses, make cups from 8cm squares of foil. Take a piece of flower paste and knead it in your hand, adding a tiny dab of white vegetable fat if it is drying out. Roll it out to 1mm thick. Using the petal cutter, cut out two or three roses. Using the ball tool, soften the edges of the petals and place into the foil cups to hold the shape of the petals. The centres are formed by the calyxes already made and a very small ball of green sugarpaste pressed with fine netting to make a criss-cross. Attach the calyx first and then the green centre using royal icing or edible glue.

Use the royal icing, or a paintbrush and edible glue, to attach the leaves, Christmas roses and berries in a wreath around the cake. Attach the ribbon with royal icing or double-sided tape. Store in a box (not an airtight container or the fridge) until ready to display.

mini christmas fruit cakes

These are a perfect gift, as they are just the right size for one person. A display of them with or without the large cake (see page 245) looks stunning as a centrepiece.

Makes 10

23cm round Chocolate Fruit
   Cake (see page 245)

4 tbsp apricot jam, warmed and
   pressed through a sieve

icing sugar, to dust

1kg marzipan

1 tbsp sherry, or cooled
   boiled water

1kg off-white/cream sugarpaste

sugarpaste decorations
   (see page 246)

TOOLS

5.5cm round cutter (3cm deep)

10 x 7.5cm round thin silver
   cake boards

a few lengths of 1–2.5cm-wide
   ribbons

Bake the chocolate fruit cake and chill overnight, to make it easier to cut. Turn the cake upside down. Using the cutter, stamp out 10 cakes; you need to be quite firm, so it doesn't crumble.

On a work top, lay out the cake boards and dab the centre of each with jam. Place a cake on each board and then, if you like, chill for an hour or so. (If the cakes are good shapes, this may not be necessary.) Brush the jam over the top and sides of each cake.

Dust a work top and rolling pin with icing sugar and roll out about 100g marzipan to 5mm thick; it needs to be larger than one cake's top and sides. Cover the cake as on page 246. Repeat until all are covered. Lightly brush the marzipan all over with sherry, then cover all the cakes with sugarpaste in the same way.

Leave overnight to firm up. You can leave the cakes now until you are ready to decorate, stored in a box (not an airtight container or the fridge or the sugarpaste will 'sweat') for a few weeks.

Decorate the cakes as on page 246 and finish with ribbons.

ginger florentines

Dark chocolate and ginger go hand-in-hand and a plate of these after dinner, or given as a gift, will always be welcomed.

Makes about 36
50g unsalted butter, in pieces
60ml double cream
60g golden caster sugar
120g flaked almonds, or
   chopped blanched hazelnuts
80g stem ginger in syrup, rinsed,
   dried and finely chopped
2 tsp plain flour
150g 70% cocoa solids
   chocolate, broken into pieces

Preheat the oven to 180°C/fan 160°C/350°F/gas mark 4. Line three large baking trays with baking parchment.

Melt the butter, cream and sugar in a small saucepan over a low heat and, once the sugar has dissolved, bring it to the boil. Remove from the heat. Crush one-quarter of the almonds roughly with your hands. Gently fold in the almonds, ginger and flour, until well combined. Place 36 half-teaspoonfuls of the mixture on to the trays, about 3–4cm apart. Flatten with a slightly damp fork.

Bake for 10–12 minutes, or until golden brown and lightly bubbling. Leave on the trays to harden for a few minutes, then remove with a palette knife to a wire rack to cool completely.

Meanwhile, melt the chocolate in a small heatproof bowl over a pan of simmering water, ensuring the bowl does not touch the water. Cool until slightly thickened.

Turn the florentines over and spread a little chocolate over the flat sides. Leave to set slightly and then, using a fork, draw wiggly lines through the chocolate. Once dry, store in an airtight tin, or pack into Kilner jars to serve over the season or give away as gifts.

winter celebration cake: chocolate and gold

A very extravagant dark, moist chocolate cake, which keeps very well so can be made a few days in advance, or frozen (though it is better to ice it on the day of eating). Perfect for a winter celebration. Halve the ingredients and bake in a 20cm round tin for 25–30 minutes to serve eight people.

The chocolate leaves can be made a day or so in advance; they are fragile so make extra!

Serves 15

FOR THE CAKE

100g dried sour cherries, roughly chopped, or dried cranberries

100ml kirsch or brandy

250g unsalted butter, in pieces, plus more for the tin

300g 70% cocoa solids chocolate, chopped

6 eggs, separated

250g light muscovado sugar or caster sugar

130g plain flour

1 tsp baking powder

pinch of salt

FOR THE CHOCOLATE ICING

150g 70% cocoa solids chocolate, chopped

200ml double cream

FOR THE DECORATION

100g 70% cocoa solids chocolate, chopped

unsprayed rose leaves, washed and dried well

small pot of pure gold leaf flecks

Preheat the oven to 170°C/fan 150°C/340°F/gas mark 3½. Soak the cherries in the kirsch overnight, or for a few hours. Lightly butter a deep 28cm round springform tin and line the base with baking parchment. Set a large heatproof bowl over simmering water, ensuring the bowl does not touch the water. Melt the chocolate and butter in the bowl, then cool a little.

Using a hand-held electric whisk, whisk the egg yolks and sugar until paler and creamy. Fold in the cooled chocolate. Sift in the flour and baking powder, tip in the cherries and Kirsch and mix. Clean and dry the whisks and whisk the egg whites with the salt to soft peaks. Take one-third and gently fold it into the chocolate mixture then, lightly, fold in the rest. Pour into the tin, smooth the top and bake for 50–55 minutes, or until a skewer comes out clean. Cool for 10 minutes in the tin, then turn on to a wire rack. When cold, turn upside down on to a large cake stand or plate.

To make the icing, melt the chocolate and cream as before. Stir until smooth. If it's too runny, let it cool for a few minutes to thicken. Spread over the top before smoothing over the sides with a palette knife. Leave to set for a couple of hours.

To make the chocolate leaves, melt the chocolate as before. Dip the backs of the leaves in the chocolate and place on a tray, chocolate-side up. When the chocolate has hardened (a spell in the fridge will help), carefully peel off the leaves. They are fragile and you may break a few, so re-melt the chocolate if necessary. Take the point of a knife and randomly place flecks of pure gold all over the cake. Finish with a circle of chocolate leaves.

A note on ingredients and equipment

Always use the very best ingredients you can afford:

Butter should be unsalted and really soft to make a great cake (unless otherwise specified). Chop it finely and soften (don't melt) in the microwave if it's cold and hard.

The size of **cake cases** can be seriously confusing. There doesn't seem to be an agreed size for the various fairy cake, muffin and cupcake cases on the market, so your baking times and yields may vary when using them.

Chocolate. I have indicated which percentage of cocoa solids I have used. But beware: this is simply a sign of strength, not of quality, exactly like wine! For milk chocolate, use at least 30% cocoa solids. White chocolate can be tricky; I use a good-quality Swiss brand.

Citrus should be unwaxed or organic, if using the zest, to avoid getting the coating wax in your cakes.

I use large, free-range or organic **eggs** and assume you will, too. They should be at room temperature.

Unbleached **flour** has more flavour, is free from chemicals and is purer. Use stoneground if possible.

Nuts. Buy little and often as they can turn rancid very quickly. Freeze any leftovers for another time.

Store **spices** in the dark, and buy small amounts, as they turn stale. Always freshly grind them when possible.

Golden **sugars** and muscovado have the best flavours. Light muscovado has a delicious fudgy taste, but save dark muscovado for gingerbreads and rich fruit cakes as it can be overpowering.

Suppliers' list

Asian ingredients
THE ASIAN COOKSHOP
www.theasiancookshop.co.uk

Bakeware and cookware (excellent, extensive ranges)
LAKELAND
www.lakeland.co.uk
015394 88100
NISBETS
www.nisbets.com
0845 140 5555

Cake and sugarcraft products
SQUIRES KITCHEN
www.squires-shop.com
0845 61 71 810
JANE ASHER
www.janeasher.com
020 7584 6177
CAKES, COOKIES & CRAFTS
www.cccshop.co.uk
01524 389684

Crystallised flowers
EAT MY FLOWERS
www.eatmyflowers.co.uk
01490 412039

Edible gold leaf
GOLD LEAF SUPPLIES
www.goldleafsupplies.co.uk
01656 720566

Metal cutters (large range, also bespoke)
FINE CUT SUGARCRAFT PRODUCTS
www.finecutsugarcraft.com
0115 933 4349

Ribbons
V V ROULEAUX
www.vvrouleaux.com
020 7224 5179

Vintage and modern kitchen accessories and glass cake stands
RE
www.re-foundobjects.com
01434 634567

Index

Acknowledgements

So many people have helped this book along its way, it is hard to know where to begin.

Firstly, very special thanks to Kishore, Hari and Tara for putting up (third time around!) with my rambling, a sticky kitchen floor and disruption all over again.

Kishore, thank you for all your valued comments, contributions and guidance throughout – even though we might not always agree!

Thank you to Martine Carter, my agent, for finding Orion, the perfect match for me.

Very special thanks to Amanda Harris at Orion for understanding the idea for the book, for your complete trust, gentle guidance and giving me the freedom to pursue it. Lucie Stericker and Kate Wanwimolruk also, for your real enthusiasm and contributions.

Miranda Harvey, designer extraordinaire, who, from the very beginning, had exactly the same vision for this book as I did – and for making it all happen.

Polly Webb-Wilson, for your beautiful styling, and Dan Jones for your quite superb photographs. I've so enjoyed working with such an exceptionally talented team.

Lucy Bannell, once more, for your patience, encouragement and answering never-ending queries. As always it's a complete delight to work with you, and thanks for editing the text so it still sounds like me!

Jacqui Pickles, thank you for sharing your expertise and for developing some of the most delicious recipes – most especially I would say the Warm Raspberry and Coconut Cake and the Cranberry and Amaretto Stollen Cake. I've so enjoyed our endless seasonal recipe debates and discussions.

Rachel Eardley: you are literally brimming full of original, creative, wonderful decorating ideas. Thanks for generously sharing your outstanding talent as always.

Lyn Hall, thank you for all your contributions along the way, and for inspiring me. It was due to you that I set out on this path all those years ago.

To Roz Denny for the Thai Rice and Coconut Cake. To my sister-in-law Gita Desai and to our mutual friend Chrissie Desopo for so generously sharing your wonderful recipes.

To Sarah Holden for so very efficiently typing a large part of this book, and Emma Joyce, too – it has been a pleasure working with both of you.

Thank you to David Trumper at Jane Asher, and to Jade Johnston and your team at the Kitchen Range Cookshop in Market Harborough, for all your assistance.

Thank you to Diana Henry for your wisdom and guidance, always given so generously.

Special thanks to all the following for all your contributions along the way, which resulted in all that washing up! Chris Adams, Emer Coyle, Molly Eardley, Liz Lowther, Louise Newton, Sally Raeder, Susanne Slack, Sarah Steele, Elle Townsend, Anna Tyler, and Joan Tyler.

First published in Great Britain in 2013 by Weidenfeld & Nicolson, an imprint of Orion Publishing Group Ltd
Orion House, 5 Upper St Martin's Lane, London WC2H 9EA
an Hachette UK company
10 9 8 7 6 5 4 3 2 1

Text copyright © Fiona Cairns 2013
Design and layout © Weidenfeld & Nicolson 2013

A CIP catalogue record for this book is available from the British Library.

ISBN: 9780297867784

Photographer Dan Jones
Designer and Art Director Miranda Harvey
Editor Lucy Bannell
Stylist Polly Webb-Wilson

Printed and bound in China

The Orion Publishing Group's policy is to use papers that are natural, renewable and recyclable products and made from wood grown in sustainable forests. The logging and manufacturing processes are expected to conform to the environmental regulations of the country of origin.

www.orionbooks.co.uk

www.fionacairns.com
twitter profile link @ fionacairns